A Mighty
Current of Grace

The Story of the Catholic Charismatic Renewal

A Mighty Current of Grace

The Story of the Catholic Charismatic Renewal

Alan Schreck

The Word Among Us Press
7115 Guilford Drive
Frederick, Maryland 21704

11 20 19 18 17   1 2 3 4 5

ISBN: 978-1-59325-309-7
eISBN: 978-1-59325-493-3

Unless otherwise noted, Scripture texts used in this work are taken from the Revised Standard Version Bible: Catholic Edition, copyright © 1965 and 1966 by the Division of Christian Education of the National Council of the Churches of Christ in the USA. All rights reserved. Used with permission.

Excerpts from the English translation of the *Catechism of the Catholic Church* for use in the United States of America, copyright © 1994, United States Conference of Catholic Bishops, Inc.—Libreria Editrice Vaticana. Used with permission.

Excerpts from documents from the Second Vatican Council are taken from *Vatican Council II, Vol. 1: The Conciliar and Post Conciliar Documents, New Revised Edition,* ed. Austin Flannery, OP (Northport, NY: Costello Publishing Company, Inc., 1998).

Cover design by Faceout Studios

Library of Congress Control Number: 2017937604

I dedicate this book to the many Spirit-filled priests who have blessed and influenced my life: Fr. Edward O'Connor, CSC; Fr. George Montague, SM; Fr. Daniel Sinisi, TOR; Fr. Angelus Migliore, TOR; Fr. Sam Tiesi, TOR; Fr. Augustine Donegan, TOR; Fr. Michael Scanlan, TOR; Fr. Giles Dimock, OP; Fr. Timothy Shannon; the Most Rev. Roger Foys; the many others who have responded to God's grace in promoting and serving the Renewal; and those who have been touched by this current of grace.

Contents

Foreword

By the Most Rev. Sam G. Jacobs
Bishop Emeritus of Houma-Thibodaux

A *Mighty Current of Grace: The Story of the Catholic Charismatic Renewal* is a gift for the Renewal as it celebrates its golden jubilee. Dr. Alan Schreck, who was part of the Renewal from its beginnings, has provided a clear and accurate oversight of the historical beginnings of this grace of the Holy Spirit and its spread among so many Catholics throughout the world. He has also traced the ebb and flow of the Renewal, with its strengths and weaknesses, from its initial vision to its present one.

Dr. Schreck recounts the impact of the Renewal in the life of the early participants and how they sought to pastor this grace according to the lead of the Holy Spirit. At the same time, he shows how the Church, through the lead of the same Holy Spirit, prepared the way for this new Pentecost and pastored it through the leadership of Cardinal Leon-Joseph Suenens, St. John XXIII, Blessed Paul VI, St. John Paul II, Pope Benedict XVI, and Pope Francis. His presentation of their thoughts and directions for this grace of the Spirit shows the concerns and support of the highest authority in our Church.

Because it was not his purpose to have an in-depth historical presentation, he was not able to include other significant pastoral initiatives of the U.S. bishops. I would like to offer two. In 1976, under the leadership of Bishop Gerard Frey of the Diocese of Lafayette, the National Conference of Catholic Bishops encouraged every diocese to appoint a liaison between the bishop and the local Renewal to provide pastoral oversight. Out of this effort came the beginnings of the Association of Diocesan Liaisons of the Catholic Charismatic Renewal, which continues today to serve their bishops in many dioceses.

The second initiative of the Conference of Bishops was the establishment of an Ad Hoc Committee for the Catholic Charismatic Renewal within the USCCB. During its continual existence until recently, this committee was able to help the other bishops in understanding the role of the Renewal. It issued several statements to the Renewal showing the support and concerns of the bishops. One of these statements, published in 1997, was entitled *Grace for the New Springtime*.

In the final chapter, Dr. Schreck outlines two scenarios of how the Renewal can have an impact on the Church in the future. The initial hope of the early participants was that the mainstream of the Church would become more reflective of the Church immediately after Pentecost. This has yet not happened. In many places, the Renewal is marginalized as another group or spirituality in the parish.

But what if the Renewal were truly understood and pastored as a current of grace for the whole Church? This is the second scenario that Schreck presents. His brief insights will be thought provoking and challenging to members of the Church who are not yet fully open to the lead of the Spirit. To those in the Renewal, it would be an answer to their dreams.

However, whatever might be written fifty years from now about the impact of the Renewal on the Church, we do know that nothing is impossible for God!

Introduction

believe in the surprises of the Holy Spirit," Cardinal Leon-Joseph Suenens once said. He certainly had good reason for this belief. As one of the four moderators of the Second Vatican Council, he witnessed the powerful action of the Holy Spirit renewing the Catholic Church in countless ways, giving the ancient Church a spiritual face-lift.

Even during the council itself, the bishops were aware of the renewal that was afoot and commented on it in their work. *Unitatis Redintegratio* [Decree on Ecumenism] notes,

> Every renewal of the Church essentially consists in an increase of fidelity to her own calling. . . . Already this renewal is taking place in various spheres of the Church's life: the biblical and liturgical movements, the preaching of the Word of God and catechetics, the apostolate of the laity, new forms of religious life and the spirituality of married life, and the Church's social teaching and activity. (6)

After the council closed, the Holy Spirit continued to act in the Church to enable it to carry out the teaching that the Spirit had inspired. Much of this happened through the established structures and agents who put church teaching into effect, such as the offices of the Roman Curia, bishops and bishops' conferences, and general chapters of religious orders.

However, less than two years after the council was adjourned, another surprise of the Holy Spirit emerged as a small seed. The Holy Spirit began to work in the lives of first dozens, then hundreds, and soon thousands of Catholics who, through a personal spiritual renewal—an encounter with Jesus Christ through the Holy Spirit—were eager to live out and promote many aspects of what the council had taught and stood for.

These Catholics desired to participate fully and actively in the liturgy, as *Sacrosanctum Consilium* [Constitution on the Sacred Liturgy] taught. They hungered for a deeper knowledge of God through reading Sacred Scripture, which *Dei Verbum* [Dogmatic Constitution on Divine Revelation] encouraged all Catholics to do. They discovered the importance and beauty of fellowship with Christians of other churches and denominations, which was the central message of *Unitatis Redintegratio*. They desired to tell others about Jesus and their own newly kindled experience of the life and the power of faith—living seeds of a "new evangelization" that Pope St. John Paul II said had begun at the Second Vatican Council. Laypeople touched by this grace wanted to be more involved and active in the mission of the Church through the use of the "charisms"—the gifts of the Holy Spirit, which were described and encouraged in *Lumen Gentium* [Dogmatic Constitution on the Church] and in *Apostolicam Actuositatem* [Decree on the Apostolate of the Laity].

And the vast majority of those affected by this surprising grace did not leave the Catholic Church or become its critics. Instead, they discovered in a new way the richness and beauty of its sacraments, its teaching (even moral teaching), and its call to a deeper communal life—a life of sharing and fellowship among Catholics who had become more alive in their faith in Christ and empowered by the Holy Spirit.

The story of this surprising (and still unfolding) work of the Holy Spirit, this mighty current of grace that came to be labeled the "Catholic Pentecostal" movement or the "Charismatic Renewal," is the subject of this book. Blessed Pope Paul VI called it a "chance" or an opportunity for the Church, and indeed it is. It is an opportunity for every Catholic, for every Christian, to discover anew "the immeasurable greatness of his power in us who believe" (Ephesians 1:19).

Alan Schreck
January 2017

Chapter 1

The Breath of God Today

Throughout her history, the Catholic Church has been
blessed with renewals—outpourings of the Holy Spirit—
that keep this ancient institution growing and vibrant. The
Holy Spirit is the secret of the Church's growth and vitality,
her fountain of youth! As the Second Vatican Council noted,
the Holy Spirit "permits the Church to keep the freshness of
youth. Constantly he renews her and leads her to perfect union
with her Spouse [Jesus]" (*Lumen Gentium,* 4).

Authentic renewal coming from the Holy Spirit does not
change or distort the nature of the Church but makes her more
vibrant and more what God intends her to be. The Second Vatican Council's *Unitatis Redintegratio* [Decree on Ecumenism]
noted, "Every renewal of the Church essentially consists in
an increase of fidelity to her own calling" (6). Catholics have
always insisted that whatever failures or weaknesses beset the
Church because of human sin, worldliness, or inertia, we never
need a new Church, for Christ founded only one Church; he
has only one Bride. However, the Church continually needs
renewal and reform, as the Second Vatican Council also stated
(*Unitatis Redintegratio,* 6).

Renewal is not the same as reform. Reform has to do with
correcting abuses and weaknesses that enter the Church due
to sin. Renewal is God's action to revitalize elements of the
Church that have been neglected or forgotten: to make the

Church "new again" or "like new." Often this renewal is God's action in which he restores or refreshes elements or aspects of the Church that we read about in the New Testament or in the writings of early Fathers of the Church.

The history of the Catholic Church is replete with countless examples of renewal, often initiated by saints or by groups and movements devoted to living out, often in a new way, some aspect of the Church's life or identity that is needed at particular times and places.[1] This book focuses on a particular renewal in the Church, the so-called Charismatic Renewal, which might also be called "Renewal in the Holy Spirit." For brevity's sake, I will simply refer to it in this book henceforth as the "Renewal."

There have been many renewals in the history of the Catholic Church similar to this one. For example, many charisms that we find in this Renewal were manifested in the poverty, or mendicant, movement initiated by Sts. Francis, Clare, and Dominic in the thirteenth century and by St. Philip Neri in Rome in the sixteenth century. Those renewals gave rise to, or infused new life into, communities in the Church: the Franciscans, the Dominicans, and the Oratory movement and communities. In the Catholic Church's history, there have been many individuals, groups, and movements characterized by particular charisms, or gifts of the Holy Spirit, that are seen in the Renewal today, such as prophecy, healing, deliverance from evil

---

1. I study these at length in my book *Rebuild My Church: God's Plan for Authentic Catholic Renewal* (Cincinnati, OH: Franciscan Media/Servant Books, 2010).

spirits, charisms of wisdom and knowledge, and even glossolalia ("speaking in tongues"). There is nothing in the present-day Renewal that is totally new or unprecedented—it is a *renewal* of the Catholic Church, not a "new" Church with unheard of or never before seen practices or phenomena. (And as we shall see, all it involves must be "tested" or discerned by the Church's leaders; see 1 Thessalonians 5:20-21.)

Yet even though there are similarities between this Renewal and other renewals and movements in the Church's history, it is not identical to any of them. That's because the Spirit of God, the Holy Spirit, always seems to bring about something fresh and new, things that in hindsight we can understand to some degree but that we never could have anticipated or predicted. Parents experience this about their child or children. Who can predict, just from knowing the gene pool of the parents, what a new human being will be like? If God can bring about such surprising newness through the procreation of human life, God certainly can be creative acting in the Church. In the Renewal, people like to talk about "surprises of the Holy Spirit," the Spirit who "blows where it wills" (John 3:8). The very existence of this Renewal, in all its various aspects and manifestations, is a "surprise" of God. And if it is a surprising work of God, should not our response be one of wonder, awe, and gratitude? Give thanks to the Lord, for he is good!

Characteristics of This Renewal

Before exploring the origins of this movement, let's briefly describe it. What distinguishes this renewal from others in Christianity, past and present? First, it is *personal*. The person "discovers" God: he enters into a new and deeper relationship with God in a way that is tailor-made for the individual person, as God wills. Second, it is *powerful*. It makes an impact on the person, conferring graces that are—at least potentially—life changing. Third, *charisms* are conferred or awakened. These are gifts given to everyone (cf. 1 Corinthians 12:7) "for the renewal and building up of the Church" and are to be "received with thanksgiving and consolation since they are fitting and useful for the needs of the Church" (*Lumen Gentium*, 12). Vatican II's *Apostolicam Actuositatem* [Decree on the Apostolate of the Laity] states further:

> From the reception of these charisms, even the most ordinary ones, there arises for each of the faithful the right and duty of exercising them in the Church and in the world for the good of men and the development of the Church, of exercising them in the freedom of the Holy Spirit who "breathes where he wills" (John 3:8). (3)[2]

Charisms are an important aspect of God's grace in this Renewal, as seen by the fact that these special graces have

---

2. All of this is also stated in the *Catechism of the Catholic Church*, 799–801.

become one name for the movement itself, i.e., the "Charismatic Renewal" or the "Charismatic movement." However, the charisms cannot be understood fully nor used to full effect without the deeper and more personal relationship with God that is also at the heart of this Renewal.

A Renewal of Pentecost

Even though most Catholics call this movement and those involved in it "charismatic," it was first known most commonly as "Pentecostal."[3] If we consider those three characteristics—personal, powerful, and the conferring of charisms—in light of what happened at Pentecost, we can understand why this renewal is called "Pentecostal." What happened at Pentecost? "They were all filled with the Holy Spirit" (Acts 2:4). The Holy Spirit came to each of Jesus' disciples gathered in the upper room in Jerusalem in a personal and powerful way that changed their lives and gave each of them charisms. They "spoke with tongues and prophesied" (Acts 19:6) and were given power to heal, cast out demons, and witness boldly to Jesus and his resurrection. Pentecost changed the lives of Jesus' followers and gave birth to, or "manifested," the Church (*Catechism of the Catholic Church*, 767). Today the Pentecostal or charismatic

---

3. The first two most widely distributed books on the Renewal were Kevin and Dorothy Ranaghan's *Catholic Pentecostals* (originally published, New York: Missionary Society of St. Paul the Apostle, 1969; revised edition published, South Bend, IN: Charismatic Renewal Services, Inc., 1983), and Fr. Edward D. O'Connor, CSC's *The Pentecostal Movement in the Catholic Church* (Notre Dame, IN: Ave Maria Press, 1971).

movement leads individuals into a personal relationship with God with spiritual power, as Jesus promised (Acts 1:8), and to reception and use of the charisms of the Holy Spirit for the service of the Church and the world. To call this grace "Pentecostal" is fitting, as it is a renewal of Pentecost.

One further word used to describe this grace also corresponds to the first Pentecost: it is a *communal* grace, in two senses. First, the grace is often received as a group of people—a community—gathers in prayer to invoke the Holy Spirit. The first Pentecost came about as a response to Jesus' command to his followers: "And behold, I send the promise of my Father [the Holy Spirit] upon you; but stay in the city, until you are clothed with power from on high" (Luke 24:49). The Book of Acts notes that "all these with one accord devoted themselves to prayer, together with the women and Mary the mother of Jesus, and with his brethren" (1:14), and "when the day of Pentecost had come, they were all together in one place" (2:1). Often in the Renewal, a community of people joins in praying with individuals that they might receive a fuller outpouring of the Holy Spirit.

Second, one of the fruits of the sending of the Holy Spirit at Pentecost is a deep desire to continue to gather, especially in prayer, and to live a communal life (see Acts 2:41-47; 4:23-35). In the present-day Renewal, the Holy Spirit continues to stir up the desire to meet together in prayer and for mutual support and fellowship. Prayer groups and committed communities are another manifestation of this Pentecostal outpouring of grace in our time.

In summary, this Renewal is rightly called "Pentecostal" because it resembles the first Pentecost in being personal, powerful, charismatic, and communal.

Origins of the Renewal

There are fascinating parallels between what was happening in Protestantism and in the Catholic Church in the mid- to late-nineteenth century that may have given rise to the Pentecostal outpouring of the Holy Spirit in the twentieth century. (I say "may" because only God knows the reasons, times, and places of his actions.)

At the same time that the "holiness movement" was growing in Protestantism (from which classical Pentecostalism emerged), an Italian religious sister named Blessed Elena Guerra, founder of the Oblate Sisters of the Holy Spirit, was writing to Pope Leo XIII and urging him to promote a more lively devotion to the Holy Spirit throughout the Catholic Church. Pope Leo responded by writing an encyclical on the Holy Spirit (*Divinum Illud Munus*) and urged all the bishops of the Church to observe the nine days between Ascension Thursday and Pentecost, the Church's original novena, with prayer in their dioceses and parishes for the outpouring of the Holy Spirit. Pope Leo himself offered a votive Mass of the Holy Ghost on the first day of the new century (January 1, 1901), petitioning the Holy Spirit to come upon the Church and the world in a new and powerful way. (Notably, that was the same day that the Pentecostal movement began, with the outpouring of the Spirit at Charles Parham's Bible School in Topeka, Kansas.)

While Pentecostalism spread and grew rapidly throughout the world, the Catholic Church seemed to be focusing on the theological struggle against modernism and on efforts for peace in a world that was engulfed in two world wars in the first fifty years of the twentieth century. The struggle against modernism created a climate in the Catholic Church that was suspicious of change and innovation.

Yet, by the time of the pontificate of Pope Pius XII, after World War II, it was clear that the Holy Spirit was doing some new things in the Catholic Church. This could be seen in papal teachings and directives, such as Pius XII's encyclical on the Church as the mystical body of Christ (*Mystici Corporis Christi*) and his cautious encouragement of Biblical scholarship, ecumenism, and liturgical reform and renewal.

There were also some things happening in the Catholic Church that were not papal initiatives but signs that God was initiating some new things in other ways. Marian apparitions occurred (such as at Fatima, Portugal) and Marian groups such as the Legion of Mary emerged. The Christian Family Movement and other spiritual associations involving the Catholic laity were formed and began flourishing. Catholic missionary activity expanded and religious communities grew. One movement that could be seen as a precursor to the Catholic Renewal of the Spirit was the Cursillo movement, founded in Spain in the 1940s by Eduardo Bonnín Aguiló. As we will discuss shortly, some of the important early leaders of the Renewal, as well as many of the men who became involved with the Renewal, either had gone on a Cursillo weekend and continued as active participants in Cursillo small groups and activities or had even worked for the Cursillo movement in some official capacity.

No Human Founder

Nearly every significant religious movement or community has a founder or founders who have some vision, idea, or plan for their work or activity that they believe is something God has called them to do. Their vision or work eventually attract people who "catch" the vision and become members or participants in the group or movement. Often we can distinguish between these founders and the leaders of the group or movement, though the founder or founders are usually the first and primary leaders.

Who founded the Catholic Charismatic Renewal/Catholic Pentecostal movement? Did any one person have a vision or an idea of starting a movement to ask the Holy Spirit to sovereignly "touch" the hearts and change the lives of Catholics and to lavish charisms upon them in abundance, as in the first Christian communities? As we shall see, there were a few people who thought this was possible and even desired it, but none of them ever claimed to be the founder of the Catholic Charismatic Renewal or were even recognized as such. I am convinced that if any individual had been called the founder of this movement, that person would have vigorously renounced the designation as being highly presumptuous. Why? Everyone involved in the beginnings of this Renewal understood that this outpouring of the Holy Spirit was a freely given, sovereign grace of God. No one had predicted that such a thing would happen among Catholics, at least not in such a massive and widespread way, much less claim to have started it.

Pope St. John XXIII called for the Church to pray that the Second Vatican Council would be a time of renewal "as though for a new Pentecost."[4] Cardinal Leon-Joseph Suenens of Belgium gave an influential speech at the council on the importance of the New Testament charisms for the Church. These were both instances of prophetic vision, but neither of these men could be called the founder of the Renewal. At most, the Renewal was something that God did in response to their prayers and vision.

Consider the beginnings of the Renewal in the United States. All of the accounts that have been written begin with some members of a student organization at Duquesne University in Pittsburgh, the Chi Rho Society, as well as a small group of faculty members there and some students and teachers at the University of Notre Dame who had connections with the people at Duquesne or in Pittsburgh. The Catholic Charismatic Renewal emerged and first spread through this network of connections and friendship among students and professors from these two schools.

God was sowing the seeds for this Renewal before its "birth" in February 1967. At Notre Dame, there was a spiritual awakening in 1963 and 1964 among a number of students, at first

---

4. John XXIII, *Humanae Salutis*, December 25, 1961, in *The Documents of Vatican II*, ed. Walter Abbott (New York: American Press, 1966), 709.

predominantly among graduate students who met to discuss issues of faith and to pray. This awakening deepened when the Cursillo movement came to South Bend through a graduate student in history, Steve Clark. A number of men from the town and campus went on a Cursillo weekend, and some, like undergraduate philosophy student Ralph Martin, experienced powerful conversions or deepening of faith in Christ. This led to their involvement in social justice issues as well as to efforts in evangelization. For example, they held "Antioch weekends" during which Notre Dame students heard a simple but powerful presentation of the gospel.

A key participant and guide for this group at Notre Dame was theology professor Fr. Edward D. O'Connor, CSC, who wrote one of the earliest books on the Renewal. He noted that before 1967, the student prayer meetings at Notre Dame were not "Pentecostal" (for example, no speaking in tongues), and they were not consistent, as students came and went. For instance, Steve Clark and Ralph Martin left Notre Dame and ended up working for the National Secretariat for the Cursillo and St. John's student parish at Michigan State University between 1965 and 1970. As mentioned earlier, the Cursillo movement was an important influence in the emergence and growth of the Catholic Charismatic Renewal. The Cursillo movement's emphasis on a personal commitment to Christ, daily prayer, and Scripture reading and fellowship provided in small-group sharing were all key marks of the Renewal as well. It is not surprising that many "Cursillistas" became involved in the Charismatic Renewal: they were open to God and hungered for more of his grace.

The Ecumenical Contribution

Why did so many Catholics become part of a movement that had started decades earlier among Protestants? And why did it happen when it did, in the mid- to late sixties? One answer is simply that it was God's will: God chose this moment in history to pour out the Holy Spirit in a new way in the Catholic Church. This is certainly true, unless one claims, at the risk of blasphemy against the Holy Spirit, that this movement is *not* from God. However, there are good reasons why God "waited" until that time in history for a renewal of Pentecost in the Catholic Church. First, in 1961 Pope St. John XXIII prayed for and asked the Church to pray for a "new Pentecost" when calling for the convocation of the Second Vatican Council. Second, that very council prophetically prepared the way for this Renewal. The council's *Unitatis Redintegratio* observed,

> Every renewal of the Church essentially consists in an increase of fidelity to her own calling. . . . Already this renewal is taking place in various spheres of the Church's life: the biblical and liturgical movements, the preaching of the Word of God and catechetics, the apostolate of the laity, new forms of religious life and the spirituality of married life, and the Church's social teaching and activity. (6)

Many members and leaders of the Renewal were laypeople or religious and priests seeking spiritual renewal. The council also prepared the way for the Charismatic Renewal by its

A Mighty Current of Grace

specific teaching on charisms, which will be discussed in chapter 3, and by calling Catholics to collaborate and seek unity with other Christians. There is a very striking section in *Unitatis Redintegratio*:

> Catholics must gladly acknowledge and esteem the truly Christian endowments for our common heritage which are to be found among our separated brethren. It is right and salutary to recognize the riches of Christ and virtuous works in the lives of others who are bearing witness to Christ, sometimes even to the shedding of their blood. For God is always wonderful in his works and worthy of all praise.
>
> Nor should we forget that anything wrought by the grace of the Holy Spirit in the hearts of our separated brethren can contribute to our own edification. Whatever is truly Christian is never contrary to what genuinely belongs to the faith; indeed, it can always bring a more perfect realization of the very mystery of Christ and the Church. (4)

Catholics can *learn* things from our "separated brethren," which can "bring a more perfect realization of the very mystery of Christ and his Church"! It is hard to imagine post-Reformation Catholics consulting Pentecostals or other Christians in order to gain insight in spiritual matters before the Second Vatican Council. But this was a key factor in the birth of the Catholic Pentecostal movement. How?

First, two paperback books—*The Cross and the Switchblade* by David Wilkerson with John and Elizabeth Sherrill

26

(1963) and *They Speak with Other Tongues* by John Sherrill (1964)—came into the hands of Ralph Martin, Steve Clark, and their friends from Duquesne, Notre Dame, and the Cursillo movement. John Sherrill had set out to observe "objectively" Pentecostal phenomena such as "baptism in the Holy Spirit" and "speaking in tongues" and ended up experiencing these phenomena himself. These books included some powerful testimonies to the power of God at work, especially Wilkerson's missionary work among street gangs in New York City, and impelled the Catholics who read them to explore further what the Holy Spirit was doing among Pentecostal Christians.

The next logical step was to contact "Spirit-filled" Pentecostal and neo-Pentecostal Christians. Since the Renewal is said to have begun in Pittsburgh, we will follow that story first. Two professors at Duquesne found an ecumenical, neo-Pentecostal prayer group led by a Presbyterian woman, Flo Dodge, that met on the north side of Pittsburgh. And there, in January 1967, these two men asked for prayer to be "baptized in the Holy Spirit." The professors were the advisors to a student organization at Duquesne, the Chi Rho Society, which was planning a student retreat in mid-February. These professors had told some friends in South Bend a week or so before this retreat weekend about their experience of being baptized in the Holy Spirit in Pittsburgh. Two of those friends were Kevin and Dorothy Ranaghan, who were soon to become leaders and witnesses to the Renewal in South Bend.

It is unusual that these two professors are seldom named in various accounts of the birth of the Renewal, because if someone wanted to identify a founder for this movement, they would be the most likely candidates. It was their experience and influence that brought about the Duquesne weekend (which will be described shortly) and that spread the news of the Pentecostal experience in the Catholic Church to Notre Dame, where it next emerged. These two Duquesne professors were Ralph Kiefer and William Storey (now both deceased). Both went on to teach at the University of Notre Dame, but neither of them was actively involved in the Renewal there (at least not as of 1970, when I became involved in the Renewal at Notre Dame as a student that spring).

The significance of Vatican II's teaching about being ready to learn from other Christians is apparent in the beginnings of the Catholic Renewal: the Duquesne professors were first exposed to the neo-Pentecostal movement and received prayer for the baptism in the Holy Spirit at a prayer meeting led by a Presbyterian woman, after having been invited there by an Episcopalian woman. And, of course, this is just the beginning of the story.

Two weeks after the Duquesne weekend, one of the Duquesne faculty members went to South Bend and witnessed to a small group of students and friends how the Holy Spirit had come in power on that weekend like a new Pentecost. On March 5, 1967, nine people, including the Ranaghans, Bert and Mary Lou Ghezzi, Gerry Rauch, Jim Cavnar, and others met and prayed to be baptized in the Holy Spirit as they had heard about from their friend the night before. Even though no one spoke in tongues or prophesied that night, they were touched by God and desired to learn more. Where could a group of Catholics go to learn more about Pentecostalism and the charisms of the Holy Spirit that they desired? To Pentecostals! I will quote the Ranaghans, who recount what happened at the home of Ray Bullard and his wife one night in March 1967:

On Monday, March 13, another group made up mostly of those who had received the baptism in the Holy Spirit and a few newcomers went to a prayer meeting in the home of an Assembly of God couple in nearby Mishawaka. He was president of the local South Bend chapter of the Full Gospel Businessmen's Fellowship International, an interfaith group of laymen who share the experience of the "baptism in the Holy Spirit." We had heard of this group and thought it good to share our experience with them. If the Pentecostal movement were merely a human fiction, or even a form of religiosity created out of the wills of men, it would have crumbled to dust that evening. Never would we have thought it possible for men and women, so radically different from one another in countless ways, to unite in the love of Christ. Yet we were united by Christ. Here we were, a group of Roman Catholics, formed in the spiritual and liturgical traditions of our church, all university-trained "intellectual types." The people with whom we were meeting were mostly from an evangelical background. They spoke with a scriptural and theological fundamentalism that was very foreign to us. Furthermore, the way they spoke and prayed, the type of hymns they sang, all this was so different that at first it was very disturbing. On the natural level these "cultural" differences were more than enough to keep us far apart from one another. Yet, in spite of these personal differences, we were enabled to come together in common faith in Jesus, in the one experience of his Holy Spirit to worship our Father together. That was no human achievement. The Holy Spirit simply cut across those cultural barriers to unite us as brothers and sisters in Christ. Many of us received that night the gift of praising God in strange languages.[5]

Even in its beginnings, we see the potential of this movement, which began originally among Protestants, to bring Catholics closer to Christians of other faith traditions, as the Second Vatican Council had urged us to do.

The Duquesne Weekend

It is widely accepted that the Renewal in the Holy Spirit began in the Catholic Church on a retreat weekend for college students sponsored by the Chi Rho Society of Duquesne University. The retreat was held on February 17–19, 1967, in the north hills of Pittsburgh, at a center named the Ark and the Dove, which is now owned by the U.S. National Service Committee of the Catholic Charismatic Renewal, which purchased it to commemorate that event.

There are a couple of striking parallels between this weekend and the beginning of the Pentecostal movement on January

---

5. Kevin and Dorothy Ranaghan, *Catholic Pentecostals Today, Revised Edition* (South Bend, IN: Charismatic Renewal Services, Inc., 1983), 23–24.

1, 1901. Both involved young people. Two professors were involved in the Duquesne weekend, and Charles Parham was a Bible teacher or pastor. At the Bible school in Topeka, Kansas, the students had been asked to study the Bible to find out all they could about being baptized in the Holy Spirit and the signs that accompanied it. This inevitably led them to focus on the Acts of the Apostles, especially the account of Pentecost—hence, the name of the movement that sprang from this event is "Pentecostal." The Chi Rho Society students going on their retreat were asked to prepare for the weekend by reading and reflecting upon the Acts of the Apostles 1–4 and David Wilkerson's *The Cross and the Switchblade,* a modern-day testimony to the power of God through baptism in the Holy Spirit. In Topeka, one young lady, Agnes Ozman, was the first to experience a powerful outpouring of the Holy Spirit, followed by others there. At the Duquesne weekend, the Holy Spirit "fell" in a powerful way upon the students on the retreat. How did it happen?

It appears that in both events, it was a sovereign act of God that no one could have planned or produced. However, in both cases, the people involved prepared for it with expectant faith—a belief, based on the testimony of the Scriptures, that God *could* act in a powerful way, that the Holy Spirit could make himself evidently present in a life-changing way, as on the day of Pentecost. (One could say that this remains the fundamental "doctrine" of the Pentecostal or charismatic movement.) This expectant faith probably began with the faith of the teachers/professors: with Charles Parham in Topeka and with Professors Storey and Kiefer, who had themselves been baptized in the Holy Spirit at the neo-Pentecostal prayer meeting they had recently attended. In having the students read the Acts of the Apostles and prepare short teachings on themes of the Holy Spirit drawn from Scripture, they revealed their hope and perhaps their expectation that God could act in a similar way in the lives of their students.

Patti Gallagher Mansfield, one of the student retreatants, observed,

> Before each presentation we sang the beautiful hymn *Veni Creator Spiritus (Come Creator Spirit)* in English, using the Gregorian chant melody. One of our professors told us Friday night that this was more than a song; it was a prayer. He wanted us to sing it repeatedly as an invocation to the Holy Spirit. It was as if he were saying, "We're going to keep on praying this until the Holy Spirit comes."[6]

However, in either case, no one could have predicted or planned how the divine action would actually happen. On the Duquesne weekend, the students had planned a birthday party for some of the retreatants on Saturday night, February 18, 1967. But one by one, a number of them were drawn to go into the chapel. The presence of God was palpable. Patti Gallagher Mansfield recalled the event:

---

6. Patti Gallagher Mansfield, *As By a New Pentecost: The Dramatic Beginning of the Catholic Charismatic Renewal, Golden Jubilee Edition* (Phoenix, AZ: Amor Deus Publishing, 2016), 71.

As we knelt there, a number of things were happening. Some people were weeping. Later they said that they felt God's love for them so intensely, they couldn't do anything but weep. Others began to giggle and laugh for sheer joy. Some people, like myself, felt a tremendous burning going through their hands and arms like fire. Others felt a clicking in their throats or a tingling in their tongues. I didn't know anything about charismatic gifts. Apparently some did pray in tongues in the chapel that night but I did not hear them. I suppose all of us could have prayed in tongues right away if we had understood how to yield to this gift. Others testify that the professors went around the room laying hands on the students there. I do not remember that anyone laid hands on me that night. As I knelt in the presence of Jesus in the tabernacle his awe inspiring presence was all that I remember.

One of the professors entered the chapel and commented, "What's the bishop going to say when he finds out that all these kids have been baptized in the Holy Spirit?" The Bishop of Pittsburgh at the time was Bishop (later Cardinal) John Wright. I heard the professor use that term, "baptized in the Holy Spirit," and I wondered what it meant. We still didn't fully realize what was happening to us, and never did we dream that what was transpiring would have an impact on the entire Church.[7]

---

7. Ibid., 80–81.

The testimonies of those on the Duquesne weekend reveal that it was not perceived in the same way by all the participants, but some of those whose lives were changed by their encounter with God that weekend, such as Patti Gallagher Mansfield and Dave Mangan, have testified powerfully to that grace for many years, even to the present.[8]

The Movement Spreads

Through a network of friends and acquaintances, news of the Duquesne weekend spread. Fr. Edward D. O'Connor, CSC, a theology professor at Notre Dame at the time, explained in his 1971 book, *The Pentecostal Movement in the Catholic Church,*

> Within a month, what had begun at Duquesne spread to the University of Notre Dame and to the Catholic student parish of Michigan State University. From these three centers it spread further, to Cleveland, to the University of Iowa, to the University of Portland (Oregon), and elsewhere. Soon people were speaking of a "Pentecostal movement" in the Catholic Church.
>
> Meanwhile similar developments were taking place in other

8. The most complete account of what happened that night is found in the Golden Jubilee Edition of Patti Gallagher Mansfield's book, *As By A New Pentecost*. The book contains the personal accounts of many who were on the Duquesne weekend and testimonies of many people prominent in the birth and early stages of the Renewal, including a 1992 testimony by the "godfather" of the Catholic Charismatic Renewal, Cardinal Leon-Joseph Suenens. He was the most prominent ecclesial spokesperson for and supporter of the movement.

parts of the country. On the east coast, in Boston and Orlando (Florida), on the west coast, in Seattle, Portland and Los Angeles, as well as in St. Louis and in central New York State, charismatic prayer groups came into being among Catholics, quite independently of those mentioned above. The majority seem to have originated about the same time as the Duquesne group, and some were definitely previous to it.[9]

Fr. O'Connor, who is a careful scholar and not prone to exaggeration, estimated that by January 1973, six years after the movement emerged, there were roughly 50,000 Catholics involved in this renewal movement in the United States and Canada. He reports that the Communication Center at Notre Dame had records of 855 prayer groups in the U.S. and 65 in Canada, with the groups having an average attendance of 40 people.[10]

The movement grew largely through person-to-person communication and interaction. One person told another what God had done in his or her own life, the effects of being baptized in the Holy Spirit. Earlier I mentioned a couple of students at Notre Dame, a graduate student, Steve Clark, and an undergrad, Ralph Martin, who had been converted to Christ on a Cursillo weekend. Later, while working for the Cursillo movement and a student parish in East Lansing, Michigan, they heard from friends about the Duquesne weekend. They traveled to Pittsburgh, where they, too, were baptized in the Holy Spirit and received the gift of tongues.

9. O'Connor, *The Pentecostal Movement in the Catholic*, 16.

10. Ibid., 16–17.

Upon returning to Michigan State, they began to tell others about their experience of the Holy Spirit. Those interested heard about a "Holy Spirit retreat" that was being held by the "charismatics" at Notre Dame on April 7–9, 1967. About forty-five people from the Lansing area arrived at Notre Dame at various hours of that Friday night. Since they outnumbered the Notre Dame people on the retreat, it was later dubbed the "Michigan State weekend." The events were held in a large classroom on the third floor of Notre Dame's Main Building (also known as the "Golden Dome"), and the climax of the retreat was the Saturday night prayer meeting, which lasted from 7:30 p.m. to the wee hours of the morning. Some members of a local Assemblies of God fellowship came to observe what was happening and joined in praying for those present to receive more of the Holy Spirit. Many testified that night and the next day that the Lord had indeed come to them in a new way. At a closing, unscheduled prayer gathering on Sunday afternoon after a closing Mass, there were manifestations of the charisms of exhortation and prophecy. Fr. O'Connor reported the gist of one prophecy: "This is only the beginning, says the Lord. You are going to see even greater works than these."[11]

It is undoubtedly true that these events were just the beginning of the Pentecostal movement in the Catholic Church. As Fr. O'Connor wrote, "The Michigan State weekend put the prayer group [at Notre Dame] into the news, and soon people started speaking of a 'Pentecostal Movement.'"[12] Passing

11. Ibid., 67.

12. Ibid.

mention of this movement among Catholics appeared in national periodicals such as *National Catholic Reporter* and in an editorial in *Our Sunday Visitor* in the spring of 1967, where it was dismissed as a strange and ephemeral fad.

Yet the "Pentecostal movement" among Catholics continued to grow, and the presence of the prayer group at Notre Dame particularly helped spread the movement, as many priests, religious, and Catholic laypeople from around the country came to Notre Dame for summer school. Beginning in the summer of 1967, many summer school students heard about the "Pentecostal movement" and attended information sessions given by the charismatic group at Notre Dame and prayer meetings on campus, where there were opportunities to be prayed over for the baptism in the Holy Spirit. Thus, the movement spread when those who had experienced the presence and power of the Holy Spirit returned to their homes or assignments.

Flowing from the Michigan State weekend and these summer prayer meetings, the Catholics involved in the Renewal at Notre Dame began to hold an annual gathering for prayer and teaching, which grew into summer conferences. The attendance more than doubled each year: beginning with 100 to 150 people in 1968, it grew to 4,500 in 1971. The 1971 conference could be called "international" because there were several foreign countries represented, as well as 147 priests and two bishops, Stephen A. Leven of San Angelo and Joseph McKinney of Grand Rapids. In 1972, there were 11,000 attendees from 16 countries. The 1973 conference had 22,000 attendees, and the general sessions were held in the Notre Dame football stadium; Cardinal Suenens was the keynote speaker that year. Attendance at the Notre Dame conference peaked at 25,000 in 1974. (I was the administrator for the 1973 and 1974 conferences. In hindsight, one of the greatest miracles of these conferences was that they came off at all, as they were largely run by college students and by volunteers who arrived just a day or two before the conference started.)

The growth of the summer conferences at Notre Dame reflected the growth of the Catholic Charismatic Renewal in the United States. The international conference of the movement in 1975 showed its growth worldwide, for it was held in Rome, Italy. The seeds of that conference were planted at a historic meeting of international leaders of the Charismatic Renewal with Pope Paul VI in Grottaferrata, Italy, in 1973. This led to the Holy Father's invitation to hold a general conference in Rome and at the Vatican on the weekend of Pentecost in 1975. Ten thousand Catholics from forty countries came to that conference. The teaching and worship sessions were held on the grounds of the Catacombs of St. Callixtus outside the city, while the two main conference Masses were held at St. Peter's Basilica, with Pope Paul VI himself as main celebrant on Pentecost Sunday and Cardinal Suenens as main celebrant on Pentecost Monday. These were truly "charismatic" Masses, with exuberant worship, praying, and singing in tongues, and some notable prophetic words were given from the pulpit of the high altar at the end of Mass. In chapter 6, we will review what Pope Paul VI said to the movement at that Mass and on other occasions. It is enough to say here that his message and attitude toward this Renewal were primarily affirming and encouraging. It is likely that the Renewal was a source of personal solace and encouragement for him during those trying times in the Church.

Taking a step back, consider how amazing it is that a movement that started among a few college students on a weekend retreat ended up just eight years later with ten thousand people from forty countries celebrating a charismatic Mass with the pope in St. Peter's Basilica, with prophecies being given at the end of Mass from the high altar. Those who attended that conference represented tens of thousands more Catholics who had been touched by the Holy Spirit through this movement around the world. Either this is a remarkable work of God's grace or, as some thought, an insidious delusion or a virulent Protestant infection in the Church. But as Jesus taught, "You will know them by their fruits" (Matthew 7:20).

What has been the most evident and significant "fruit" of this movement? I would say that it is changed lives. And what begins that change for nearly everyone in this Renewal is, in the term most commonly used in the Renewal, "baptism in the Holy Spirit." What that means is the subject of the next chapter.

Chapter 2

Baptism in the Holy Spirit

A Grace for the Church

I was an incoming freshman at the University of Notre Dame in the fall of 1969 when an upper classman who lived on the same floor of my dorm approached me one day and invited me to attend a "prayer meeting" off campus.

"What's a prayer meeting?" I asked, and after he had explained that a group of students and faculty just met to worship God in a free and spontaneous way, including sometimes praying in strange, unknown languages, my second question, naturally, was "Is it really Catholic?"

His answer was to pull out a Bible from his jacket and show me where in the Bible it mentioned worshipping "in the Spirit" and "praying in tongues." Since I knew that Catholics believed in the teaching of the Bible, I agreed to go with him to this prayer meeting. I probably never would have considered it except that I had been grappling with some pretty fundamental questions, such as "Is God real?" and "If God is real, how do I *know* this?" I never stopped going to Mass and had even started going to Friday night meditation/socials at an Opus Dei house near campus. But because I was still searching for something—for some answers or just for God to "show" himself—I was open to going to the prayer meeting, in spite of some reservations.

When I went to the meeting, held in the living room of Notre Dame physics professor Paul DeCelles and his wife, Jeanne, I was immediately struck by the friendliness of the group and, most of all, by the way they talked about God. They spoke about "the Lord" freely and as if they knew God personally.

This was quite unlike anything I had experienced before. The worship was joyful and spontaneous and included people reading passages from the Bible, speaking out with a "word from the Lord," and sometimes praying and singing in words that were not English. Although it was totally strange to me, again I was struck that these people "knew" God in a way that I didn't. They truly believed that God was actually present in their midst, speaking to them and listening to their prayers. Later, in an explanation session before another prayer meeting, I learned that what had first opened up many of them to know God in this way was being "baptized in the Spirit."

Meanwhile, the spiritual struggle and darkness I had been experiencing that year became more intense. I had been meeting weekly with an Opus Dei priest who tried to answer all my questions about God, but finally he told me that he thought my issues were deeper than simply intellectual questions. I knew he was right. I would stop randomly in dorm chapels between classes and beg God, if he were real, to show himself to me. I kept going to the prayer meetings and went to some additional explanation sessions as part of what was called "Life in the Spirit." Realizing how much I needed God, if he were real, to intervene in my life, finally I asked the leaders of the prayer group to pray for me to receive this "baptism in the Holy Spirit." The prayer group had outgrown the DeCelles' living room and the meetings were now being held in the basement of St. Joseph's Elementary School. After the meeting one night, a group of us went up to the auditorium, and I, with some others, prayed together to receive a fuller outpouring of the Holy Spirit.

That prayer totally changed my life. Later that night, as I walked around the Notre Dame campus with another guy who had also received prayer, I felt an indescribable peace and joy. I knew God was real and was with me. Before I went to bed, I told the Lord that I was afraid that I might think later that this was just an emotional "high." So I asked him to give me a sign that it wasn't. I had heard that sometimes people would pray and open their Bible at random and God would give them a passage that would "speak" to them and their situation. I prayed, "Lord, I am not superstitious, but you know how much I need to know that this night is truly a blessing from you and not just a passing feeling. Please show me that this is your Holy Spirit acting in me." When I opened the Bible, my eyes fell on a passage about the sending of the Holy Spirit. But I needed to know that this was not just a coincidence, so I asked the same thing again, and again I opened to another passage about the Holy Spirit. Then, feeling a little like Abraham when he kept calling upon God to spare Sodom from destruction, or like Gideon praying about the dew on the fleece, I prayed a third time: "Lord, please just show me one more time that this is your Holy Spirit." Again, I opened to a third passage about the Holy Spirit being given. I fell into bed that night, and I still remember that I couldn't stop smiling as

I lay there, giving thanks to God. My "search" for God was over. The Hound of Heaven had captured his prey.

I don't relate this personal testimony because it is normative—what "ought to happen" to everyone. On the contrary, my story illustrates how personal God's action is. The Lord knows what each person needs in his or her journey toward him. It seems that the most important factors that matter in seeking this grace of baptism in the Holy Spirit are hunger for God and openness to him and his action. However, the Holy Spirit acts freely; some people receive an outpouring of the Holy Spirit or particular gifts of the Spirit in ways that are totally unexpected, like St. Paul's encounter with Jesus on the road to Damascus (see Acts 9:1-19).

My wife's contact with the Renewal at the University of Michigan at about the same time as mine was similar. She was searching for God. Although her family was only very nominally Protestant, she had been confirmed in the Lutheran Church and attended services at the Lutheran student center near campus, trying to figure out where and if God fit into the world. A group of Lutheran students who went to church at the center also went to "Pentecostal" prayer meetings at the Catholic student center. One young woman in particular invited Nancy to attend a prayer meeting. She didn't really give her much information about it.

When she went to the prayer meeting, Nancy listened to the young people around her talking about "the Lord" in a personal way, unlike anything she had previously experienced. In the course of the meeting, she "felt" known and loved uniquely, and she sensed that God was awaiting a response. Remembering a sermon she once heard about a famous picture with Jesus knocking on the handleless door of our hearts, she imagined a door within her and opened it. At the end of the prayer meeting, as she went upstairs to a small group, she wondered exactly what she was thinking and feeling. The small group was part of an ongoing Life in the Spirit Seminar. Four weeks later, she asked for and received prayer to be baptized with the Holy Spirit. She became an active member of the prayer community and, through contact with many fervent, joyful Catholics, a few years later entered the Catholic Church.

Our stories are typical of how the Renewal spread on college campuses in its early years. One student told another about his or her own experience or about a prayer meeting that was happening on or near campus.

Life in the Spirit Seminars

Both my wife and I were introduced to the new Pentecostal movement and its gateway, baptism in the Holy Spirit, by attending a Life in the Spirit Seminar in 1970. The original format of this seminar was developed by leaders of the Renewal in Ann Arbor, Michigan.[1]

In this book's first chapter, we saw how Steve Clark and Ralph Martin became involved in the Renewal in its earliest stages at Notre Dame and eventually were employed by the National Secretariat of the Cursillo. The Cursillo movement had profound pastoral wisdom on how to lead people to conversion through a carefully designed retreat and how to enable those converted to grow and to persevere in their new or renewed Christian faith through ongoing support groups.

When God began pouring out the Holy Spirit in a new way, "baptizing" people with a new outpouring of the Holy Spirit, Clark and Martin sought to develop a pastoral approach to enable these people to grow more fully in their relationship with God and in their Christian life. Out of this came the Life in the Spirit Seminars. The purpose of these seminars is explained in the introduction of the first and second editions of the *Team Manual,* published in 1971 and 1972, respectively:

> Over the past four or five years, we have been actively engaged
> in seeking God's will about how to help people be baptized
> in the Spirit and find a deeper Christian life. The Lord has

1. Stephen Clark's name is on the cover of the first and second editions of the *Team Manual for the Life in the Spirit Seminars* (Notre Dame, IN: Charismatic Renewal Services, Inc., 1971, 1972). However, the preface to the 3rd (Revised) Edition (1973) states, "The Life in the Spirit Seminars have always been the product of a team effort. They were originally developed by a team of people working under Ralph Martin in The Word of God in Ann Arbor, Michigan. The first edition of the *Team Manual* came from that original effort" (1).

been constantly emphasizing to us that we cannot consider baptism in the Spirit apart from the rest of the Christian life. We cannot consider it an extra, added attraction to the Christian life—something like a set of Sunday clothes which you bring out on special occasions (prayer meetings, for instance). Rather, baptism in the Spirit is the entry into a fuller life of the Spirit, and our life in the Spirit should be expressed in daily Christian living.[2]

It is important to see here how the early leaders of the Renewal movement understood God's purpose in this outpouring of the Holy Spirit. They saw God's *primary* purpose, not as giving a spiritual experience or particular charisms, but as calling people to live a dedicated Christian life. Baptism in the Holy Spirit is the *means* by which God is calling people to this life, and the charisms, as we shall see, are what God has provided to equip people to carry out their mission in the Church and the world. Baptism in the Spirit is the "jump start" enabling people to begin to live a full Christian life as it is presented in the Bible and ancient Christian tradition.

The manual goes on to explain how the leaders of the prayer meeting discovered that people would open up to the work of the Spirit if they were prayed with at a time and place separate from the prayer meeting itself. At first, the leaders simply explained the baptism in the Spirit and prayed with those open to receiving it in another room. Later, the leaders realized that

---

2. *Team Manual for the Life in the Spirit Seminars*, Second Edition (Notre Dame, IN: Charismatic Renewal Services, Inc., 1972), 3.

they needed to provide more careful instruction, introducing people "to life in the Spirit, and not just 'the baptism in the Spirit.' We would have to teach them how to begin a consistent relationship with Christ in the power of the Spirit."[3] They learned that by taking the emphasis off the spiritual experience of being baptized in the Spirit and putting it instead on living a new life in the Spirit, people would have more success both in opening up to the Lord and in persevering in the Christian life.

The Life in the Spirit Seminars are teachings designed to help people understand what baptism in the Spirit is and to put it in the context of God's plan of salvation, the call to be a disciple and an active member of his body, the Church. It is noteworthy that the topics addressed in the seven seminar talks have not changed since the first edition in 1971: God's Love; Salvation; The New Life; Receiving God's Gift; Praying for Baptism in the Holy Spirit; Growth; and Transformation in Christ. In other words, the authors of the seminars wished to present the work and grace of the Holy Spirit in its proper context: God's plan of salvation and the Holy Spirit's role in the life of a Christian and of the Church.

An Ecumenical Grace

It is important to note that even though Clark, Martin, and many of those who developed these seminars were Catholic, they understood that this grace of baptism in the Holy Spirit

---

3. Ibid., 4.

in modern times had been lavished upon Christians of many different churches and denominations. Since the turn of the twentieth century, it has been an ecumenical grace. The prayer group in Ann Arbor, Michigan, which developed into a covenant community, was also ecumenical, and members of the team who developed and conducted the seminars were from various Christian backgrounds, as this paragraph from the introduction to the first two editions of the *Team Manual* attests to:

> The Life in the Spirit seminars are designed to be universal. They were originally developed in a community that is a majority Catholic but that contains a high percentage of other Christians from conservative Fundamentalist to "high church" Lutheran and Episcopalian. We long ago had to learn to present the basic message in such a way that it could be received by every type of Christian. Surprisingly enough, we found that it could be done. All of us want to say more about the Christian life than is contained here. But all of us agree that what is said here is true and is adequate to lead people to be baptized in the Spirit and to speak in tongues. Our hope is that The Life in the Spirit Seminars can be used by a broad spectrum of Christians and will prove to be unifying throughout the Charismatic Renewal.[4]

The twentieth century was a time of increased dialogue and efforts toward unity among Christians, and for Catholics, the Second Vatican Council's *Unitatis Redintegratio* was

4. Ibid., 5–6.

a landmark document in which Catholics began assuming greater responsibility and even leadership in the movement toward Christian unity. The Holy Spirit is the ultimate source of unity, both within the blessed Trinity and in all of God's activity outside of himself, so the grace of baptism in the Holy Spirit sweeping through the Catholic Church was a powerful, divine impetus toward unity.

I vividly remember one day in 1971 when I was waiting with friends in the lunch line in the cafeteria at Notre Dame. An older, white-haired couple joined us; they had been introduced to us because we were members of the fledgling Catholic charismatic community on campus. They were very kind and polite and listened intently as we talked about our experience of being baptized in the Spirit and our life and worship as Catholic students belonging to a Pentecostal group. Later, we learned that the gentleman, David du Plessis, was known around the world as "Mr. Pentecost"—one of the most prominent Pentecostal leaders in the world and a strong advocate of Christian unity. He had come to Notre Dame to see for himself what the Holy Spirit was doing among Catholics.

Many Pentecostals, especially in those early days of "Catholic Pentecostalism," simply could not believe that Catholics could be baptized in the Holy Spirit and receive spiritual gifts such as speaking in tongues and prophecy. Through this movement, God has begun to change minds and hearts of Catholics, Pentecostals, and other Christians, tearing down walls of misunderstanding and prejudice that have kept us apart. There is still much more to be done, but God's action of granting this particular grace of the Holy Spirit to *all* Christians provides a common experience that can be a starting point for discussion and prayer together, as *Unitatis Redintegratio* urges Catholics and all Christians to pursue.

What Is "Baptism in the Holy Spirit"?

This book is not a theological study but a look at the history of the Renewal of the Holy Spirit among Catholics. Yet this history, to be complete, must include how Catholics have variously sought to explain the meaning of the fundamental characteristics of this Renewal, beginning with being "baptized in the Holy Spirit."

First, we must ask, "Why was this phrase used by Catholics to refer to their powerful, life-changing experience of God?" The answer is that Pentecostals and, later, neo-Pentecostals used this phrase. They did so because it was biblical: John the Baptist says that Jesus would baptize in the Holy Spirit, and Jesus, in a post-resurrection appearance, "charged them not to depart from Jerusalem, but to wait for the promise of the Father, which, he said, 'you heard from me, for John baptized with water, but before many days you shall be baptized with the Holy Spirit'" (Acts 1:4-5). This promise was fulfilled at Pentecost.

Thus, Pentecostal Christians speak of a person's own powerful, life-changing encounter with God as being "baptized in the Holy Spirit." So it is not surprising that Catholics in the beginnings of the Renewal, who heard about this experience from Pentecostals and neo-Pentecostals and had read books by

Wilkerson and Sherill, who both used this terminology, naturally adopted it to describe their own powerful experience of God.

Very soon, Catholics with some theological training began to ask whether speaking of "baptism in the Holy Spirit" or being "baptized in the Spirit" was proper and acceptable for Catholics and also, regardless of the terminology, how this experience of God was to be understood by Catholics. Specifically, they sought to understand how it was related to two of the sacraments of initiation: baptism and confirmation. The first edition (1969) of *Catholic Pentecostals* by Kevin and Dorothy Ranaghan observed, "If we were to be more precise we would not talk of receiving the Baptism in the Holy Spirit, but of renewing the Baptism in the Spirit."[5]

Others have proposed different names that they believe more accurately describe the Pentecostal experience, as a document produced following a meeting of Catholic theologians in Malines, Belgium, in 1974 observed,

> In France *'l'effusion de l'Esprit'* is more generally used; *'Firmerneuerung'* is used in Germany. Some English-speaking countries speak of 'the release of the Spirit'. . . . Care should be take that in the pursuit of an alternate or preferred vocabulary that which is essential to the charismatic renewal not be filtered out when the phrase 'baptism in the Holy Spirit' is set aside. Whatever the terminological decisions of each country, it is important that all be saying the same thing, namely that the power of the Holy Spirit,

5. Ranaghan and Ranaghan, *Catholic Pentecostals*, 151.

given in Christian initiation but hitherto unexperienced, becomes a matter of personal conscious experience.[6]

Thankfully, these different terms have not caused any major rift in the Catholic Charismatic Renewal over the past fifty years. Nor have the differences in the theological understanding of this contemporary outpouring of the Holy Spirit produced any actual division in the Renewal. This should not be taken for granted: the Pentecostal movement at the turn of the twentieth century eventually broke into many distinct groups/churches/denominations, and one cause of this was conflict over the interpretation of "baptism in the Spirit" and related theological issues. Hence, it is a special gift of God and a work of the Holy Spirit, the Spirit of unity, that issues of terminology and theological understanding have not caused divisions among Catholics in this worldwide spiritual renewal. Perhaps this is because there has been continual, open discussion of it among Catholic theologians involved in the movement and with bishops and other pastoral leaders since the Renewal's emergence in the Catholic Church.

Approaches to Understanding "Baptism in the Holy Spirit"

How have Catholics come to understand this contemporary experience of being "baptized in the Holy Spirit"? Over the

---

6. *Theological and Pastoral Orientations on the Catholic Charismatic Renewal* (Notre Dame, IN: Word of Life, 1974), 33. This will hereafter be referred to as "Malines Document I."

past fifty years, Catholic theologians (joined with other Christian thinkers) have sought to interpret this outpouring of the Holy Spirit within a Catholic framework. I will briefly summarize the main Catholic views of how being "baptized in the Holy Spirit" may be understood today within this Renewal, but those who are interested can learn more in the appendix.

1. It refers to a release, actualization, or coming to conscious awareness of the presence, power, and gifts of the Holy Spirit that are received in baptism and confirmation. This is especially important for those who have received these sacraments as infants or children and for those whose catechesis did not adequately prepare them to expect and understand the fullness of life in Christ and in the Spirit that is conferred in these sacraments. Most Catholic theologians teach some form of this understanding.

2. It is expressed in the teaching of St. Thomas Aquinas as a "grace freely given" by God (*gratia gratis datae)* to enable a person to perform a new ministry or undertake a fuller, more radical expression of Christian life; or, from another section of St. Thomas Aquinas, it is a grace that removes obstacles to a full, normal living of Christianity in the power of the Holy Spirit (conferred in sacramental baptism) as this is described in the New Testament and by many early Christian writers.

3. It is a sign that we are entering into a period of world evangelization and crisis that Jesus teaches will precede his Second

Coming, though we do not know the time of his return. This is an eschatological understanding based on the increasing worldwide extent of baptism in the Spirit.

4. It is a personal revelation to the believer of the Lordship of Jesus Christ—the Holy Spirit making Jesus and the Father known to us in a personal way, leading to conversion, openness to the gifts of the Spirit, and openness to the Spirit's work of sanctification/holiness.

What is important to stress here is that, beginning in May 1969, Catholic theologians involved in or sympathetic to this movement have met frequently to discuss the Pentecostal phenomena in the Catholic Church. As we shall see later, these early theological discussions laid the groundwork that encouraged the Catholic magisterium to make statements largely supportive of the Catholic Pentecostal movement.

One of the regular participants at these meetings, Fr. Kilian McDonnell, OSB, then executive director of the Institute for Ecumenical and Cultural Research in Collegeville, Minnesota, noted,

> This theological concern did not ensure that Catholic Pentecostalism would avoid all the pitfalls to which an enthusiastic movement is liable, but it did give the movement the kind of theological stability which was not present at the beginnings of classical Pentecostalism and Protestant neo-Pentecostalism.[7]

---

7. Kilian McDonnell, OSB, *Catholic Pentecostalism: Problems in Evaluation* (Pecos, NM: Dove Publications, 1970), 23.

So, what did these Catholic theologians have to say about this Pentecostal movement and "baptism in the Spirit"? In the same book, Fr. McDonnell noted,

> Because Pentecostalism is not a denomination, not a doctrine, but a spirituality, an experience, a way of life, which has a scriptural basis, it can fit into a Roman Catholic, a Lutheran, a Presbyterian context. Its central concern, once again, is fullness of life in the Holy Spirit and the exercise of all the gifts. A decisive moment in this fullness of life is the baptism in the Holy Spirit. The vocabulary here is taken over from Acts 1:4, 5: "He charged them not to depart from Jerusalem, but to wait for the promise of the Father, which, he said, 'you heard from me, for John baptized with water, but before many days you shall be baptized with the Holy Spirit.'"[8]

One point of difference, he explained, is whether speaking in tongues is a necessary sign or "evidence" of being baptized in the Holy Spirit: classical Pentecostals say yes, while "Catholic Pentecostals almost universally reject the necessary link between the baptism [in the Spirit] and speaking in tongues."[9] However, he added, one of the most important results or "fruits" of being baptized in the Holy Spirit, according to Catholic Pentecostals, is a deepening of their prayer life. Fr. McDonnell noted that Catholic Pentecostals have a hunger to pray, and praise becomes the basic orientation of their prayer; speaking

8. Ibid., 17.

9. Ibid., 18.

in tongues is experienced as a gift that enhances their prayer life, especially in praise and intercession.[10]

A Contemporary Presentation of Baptism in the Spirit

The many years of research, discussion, and debate about "baptism in the Spirit," as it has been called and experienced in the Catholic Church, led to a document entitled *Baptism in the Holy Spirit* that was published in 2012 by the Doctrinal Commission of the International Catholic Charismatic Renewal Services (ICCRS). The drafting of the document began in 2008, but the final discussion and review occurred in Rome in March 2011 at an International Colloquium on Baptism in the Holy Spirit under the patronage of the Pontifical Council for the Laity. One hundred fifty leaders from forty-four countries participated in the colloquium. Fr. Raniero Cantalamessa, OFM Cap, preacher of the papal household, was one of the participants and a main presenter. The key authors of the text were Dr. Mary Healy (Sacred Heart Major Seminary, Detroit) and Msgr. Peter Hocken (England/Austria). Although the final published document does not have *magisterial* authority, it was produced at the request of both ICCRS and the Pontifical Council for the Laity.

The document consists of theological reflections and comments on pastoral issues. Some of the reflections are inspirational:

---

10. Ibid., 19–20.

Through baptism in the Spirit Pentecost is made present and alive in the Church today. To be baptized in the Holy Spirit is to be filled with the Love that eternally flows between Father and Son in the Holy Trinity, a love that changes people at the deepest level of their being and makes them capable of loving God in return.[11]

Other statements in this document seek to interpret the phenomenon theologically and include all of the different interpretations mentioned above. Baptism in the Spirit is "an actualization of the sacraments of initiation, a 'fanning into flame' the gift already received (cf. 2 Timothy 1:6)" in baptism and confirmation.[12] It also may be seen as "the Spirit of God coming in a new way into a person's life and bestowing new gifts, . . . a fuller release of the Spirit and his charisms, especially in preparation for a new mission or task to which God is calling them."[13] It is also seen as "a revelation of the Father's love and of the truth that 'Jesus is Lord.' . . . It is a surrender to Jesus' lordship through the Holy Spirit, so that one is increasingly 'led by the Spirit of God' (Romans 8:14)."[14]

However, when the question is asked, "Is baptism in the Spirit for every Christian?" the answer given is based on the majority view that baptism in the Spirit is a "release" or

11. Doctrinal Commission of ICCRS, *Baptism in the Holy Spirit* (Locust Grove, VA: NSC Chariscenter, 2012), 65.

12. Ibid., 71–72.

13. Ibid., 72–73.

14. Ibid., 68.

"actualization" or "conscious awareness" of what is received in the sacraments of initiation:

> Baptism in the Spirit is for all the baptized insofar as it is coming alive of sacramental baptism and confirmation.
>
> Similarly, charisms as such are for the whole Church, since they belonged to the ministry of Jesus and were part of what he passed on to the Church through the Twelve.[15]

In light of this, is the Charismatic Renewal just "a movement among other movements in the Church, with its own particular style and spirituality"? The answer is yes *but* with a necessary qualification: *if* it is *normative* for baptized Christians to know, experientially, what it means that Jesus is Lord of their lives and to experience the power and presence of the Holy Spirit, including the charisms that God has given them, *then* "the Renewal is unique, in that it is the bearer of a grace that belongs to the whole Church and is meant for the renewal of the whole Church."[16]

Thus, the widespread experience of the power and presence of God among Christians that is called "baptism in the Holy Spirit" is seen by those in this Renewal as a *gift* of God and as an important *message* of God to the whole Church—to *all* followers of Christ—that says, "I want you to know me, and to know (or to know more fully) the reality and the power of my presence in your lives. I also want you to receive and use all

15. Ibid., 75.

16. Ibid., 89.

the gifts I have for you for the service of others and the building up of my Church." This, I believe, is what God is speaking to the Church through this prophetic current of grace.

Chapter 3

Charisms of Word and Worship

I t is not by chance that the name most commonly attached to this Renewal and its adherents is "charismatic." But what does this mean? What are "charisms," and why should a movement in the Church focus on them?

St. Paul uses two Greek words to refer to these same "gifts of the Spirit," or "charisms." One of them, *charismata,* simply means "gifts," and the other, *pneumatika,* literally means "things of the Spirit" or "manifestations of the Spirit." Both terms refer to gifts that God confers on each Christian to build up the Church, the body of Christ (see 1 Corinthians 12:7). When St. Paul presents his most comprehensive list of these charisms in 1 Corinthians 12:1-11, he states that these are gifts that come from the Holy Spirit: "All these are inspired by one and the same Spirit, who apportions to each one individually as he wills" (verse 11). St. Paul then presents the analogy, which he originated, of the Church as the "body of Christ." These charisms are likened to different parts of the human body (the eye, ear, hand, and so forth), which differ in function but which are all essential for the human body to function properly (1 Corinthians 12:14-26).

St. Paul also associates these charisms with various "offices," or tasks, in the Church: "Now you are the body of Christ and individually members of it. And God has appointed in the church first apostles, second prophets, third teachers, then workers of miracles, then healers, helpers, administrators, speakers in various kinds of tongues" (1 Corinthians 12:27-28). Similar lists of charisms are given in Ephesians 4:11 and Romans 12:4-11. The list in Romans includes gifts of service, exhortation, giving aid, giving money, and doing acts of mercy. St. Peter also refers to those charisms in his first letter: "As each has received a gift, employ it for one another, as good stewards of God's varied grace: whoever speaks, as one who utters oracles of God; whoever renders service, as one who renders it by the strength which God provides" (4:10-11). Note that in every case, these charisms are given primarily to provide service to others.

So what is the place of these charisms in the life of the Church? Are they essential to Christianity, that is, part of what it means to be Catholic? Or are they "optional"—perhaps one of the distinctive aspects of particular movements, groups, or religious orders in the Church, but not for everyone? Sts. Peter and Paul seem to indicate that they are for everyone: *each* has received a gift for building up the Church (1 Corinthians 12:7; 1 Peter 4:10).

The Game Changer

If asked what role charisms played in the life of the Church today, prior to 1960 most Catholics, including most bishops and priests, would have said, "None" or "Very little"—if they even understood the term "charisms" at all in its biblical usage. Some more theologically informed might have explained that charisms were present in early Christianity but were later subsumed into the Church's ordained ministry or have appeared occasionally in the lives of the saints. The Second Vatican Council changed all that—or at least that was the intent. When the bishops at the council were developing what turned out to be the council's central document, *Lumen Gentium* [the Dogmatic Constitution on the Church], a commission formulated a draft for the bishops to review. One of the four moderators of the council, Cardinal Leon-Joseph Suenens, the primate of Belgium at the time, observed that there was something missing in its description of the constitution of the Church: there was no mention of the charisms discussed by Sts. Peter and Paul. He proceeded to address the council with a speech entitled "The Charismatic Dimension of the Church":

> The remarks made about the charisms of the Christian people are so few that one could get the impression that charisms are nothing more than a peripheral and unessential phenomenon in the life of the Church. Now the vital importance of these charisms for building up the Mystical Body must be presented with greater clarity and consequently at greater length. What is to be completely avoided is the appearance that the hierarchical structure of the Church appear as administrative apparatus with no intimate connection with the charismatic gifts of the Holy Spirit which are spread throughout the life of the Church.

> The time of the Church, which is on pilgrimage through the centuries until the Parousia of the Lord, is the time of the Holy Spirit.[1]

The speech was not long. He briefly reviewed the New Testament teaching on the charisms and insisted that they were not just a feature of the Church in biblical times but that they were equally important today as well and belonged by right to every member of the Church: "It was not in past ages alone, not only in the time of St. Thomas Aquinas or St. Francis Assisi that the Church was in need of the charisms of prophets and other ministries; she needs them today as well and needs them in her ordinary everyday life."

He also urged pastors to be open to and to encourage these gifts of the Holy Spirit, including those given to laypeople.

This speech could have been just one of the thousands of interventions addressed to the council and forgotten, but instead, its teaching on the nature and use of charisms in the Church was incorporated into at least three council documents:

> Allotting his gifts according as he wills (cf. 1 Corinthians 12:11), he also distributes special graces among the faithful of every rank. By these gifts he makes them fit and ready to undertake various tasks and offices for the renewal and building up of the Church, as it is written, "the manifestation of the Spirit is given to everyone for profit" (1 Corinthians 12:7).

---

1. Cardinal Leon-Joseph Suenens, "The Charismatic Dimension of the Church" (speech, Second Vatican Council, Vatican City, October 22, 1963).

Whether these charisms be very remarkable or more simple and widely diffused, they are to be received with thanksgiving and consolation since they are fitting and useful for the needs of the Church. (*Lumen Gentium,* 12)

From the reception of these charisms, even the most ordinary ones, there arises for each of the faithful the right and duty of exercising them in the Church and in the world for the good of men and the development of the Church, of exercising them in the freedom of the Holy Spirit who "breathes where he wills" (John 3:8), and at the same time in communion with his brothers in Christ, and with his pastors especially. (*Apostolicam Actuositatem,* 3)

While trying the spirits if they be of God (cf. 1 John 4:1), [priests] must discover with faith, recognize with joy, and foster with diligence the many and varied charismatic gifts of the laity, whether these be of a humble or more exalted kind. (*Presbyterorum Ordinis* [Decree on the Ministry and Life of Priests], 9)

What was at stake here was not just the council's recognition of charisms and their inclusion in these documents. There was also new light being shed on a fundamental understanding of the Church. Is the Church primarily a hierarchically structured institution that Jesus established, composed of offices of leadership with defined authority? Or is the Church a community of believers, who each have one or more of a variety of gifts (charisms) given by God for the Church to function and carry out her mission in the world? Posed in this way, it appears to be an either/or question, but the answer given by the Second Vatican Council was "both!" In *Lumen Gentium,* the Church is acknowledged as both "the community of faith, hope, and charity" and a visible organization [i.e., institution] through which "[God] communicates truth and grace to all men." It continues:

> But, the society structured with hierarchical organs and the mystical body of Christ, the visible society and the spiritual community, the earthly Church and the Church endowed with heavenly riches, are not to be thought of as two realities. On the contrary, they form one complex reality which comes together from a human and a divine element. (*Lumen Gentium,* 8)

The "institutional, hierarchical" church and the "charismatic, spiritual" church are the same church, the one Church of Christ. The Church is an institution, but it is a charismatic institution.

The impact of this new understanding of the Church is evident in a talk given by Cardinal Joseph Ratzinger (later Pope Benedict XVI) in 1998. He explained that the basic structural or institutional element of the Church—the basis of the hierarchical order of the Church—is *ordo,* the Sacrament of Holy Orders. However, he pointed out that the basis of ordination is actually a *charism*—a gift (or gifts) of God. God's call to Holy Orders is a gift; the things that qualify a person to receive this sacrament are also gifts (the charisms of pastor, teacher, and, in the case of bishops, apostle), and what is received in the sacrament itself is new gifts or a strengthening of the charisms the person already possesses for the service of others and the Church.[2]

Even though the offices of the Church that are the basis of the Church as a hierarchically structured institution—bishop, priest, and deacon—*seemed* to replace the charisms of apostle, prophet, pastor, and teacher, their ministry is in fact based on these charisms.

So what is the purpose (hopefully God's purpose) of the Renewal with regard to these charisms? Why does the Church

---

2. Cardinal Joseph Ratzinger, "The Ecclesial Movements: A Theological Reflection on Their Place in the Church," in *Movements in the Church: Proceedings of the World Congress of the Ecclesial Movements* (Vatican City: Pontificum Consilium Pro Laicis, 1999), 25–26. Cardinal Ratzinger observed: "But if we try to elucidate the two concepts, in order to arrive at valid rules for defining their mutual relationship, something unexpected happens. The concept of 'institution' falls to bits in our hands as soon as we try to give it a precise theological connotation. For what, after all, are the fundamental institutional factors that characterize the Church as the permanent organizational structure of her life? The answer is, of course, the sacramental ministry in its different degrees: bishop, priest, deacon. The sacrament that, significantly, bears the name *Ordo*, is, in the last analysis, the sole permanent and binding structure that forms so to say the fixed order of the Church. It is the sacrament that constitutes the Church as an 'institution.' . . . Only secondarily is the sacrament realized through a call on the part of the Church. But primarily it comes into being by God's call, that is to say, only at the charismatic and pneumatological level. It can only be accepted and lived by virtue of the newness of the vocation and by the freedom of the *pneuma*."

need a "charismatic" renewal? One purpose is certainly to strengthen and expand the charisms possessed by the Church's ordained ministers—to encourage those in Holy Orders to rely more on the gifts, power, and guidance of the Holy Spirit in their ministries. The other purpose is to make *all* of the members of the Church aware of their need to be open to these charisms and to *use* the gifts they receive for God's glory, to deepen and strengthen their own Christian lives and to serve others more effectively.

Therefore, the charisms are not just a fad, a "new toy," or a spiritual diversion only for some Catholics. ("Let's go to the prayer meeting so we can speak in tongues, prophesy, pray for healing, get a 'word' from the Lord.") According to the New Testament and the Second Vatican Council, charisms are not just an "extra" or an "add-on" to normal, "ordinary" Catholic life. The council indicates that charisms are as essential to the life of a Catholic as the sacraments and following the teachings of the bishop and pastor (*Lumen Gentium*, 12).

Pope St. John Paul II, based on this teaching of Vatican II, taught that the charisms are "co-essential" with the sacraments and the ministry of the Church's ordained ministers in the Church's constitution.[3] In other words, if we were to list adjectives that properly describe the Catholic Church, we could say that the Church is sacramental, Eucharistic, Marian, pro-life, and concerned for the poor; we could also say that

3. John Paul II, Speech of the Holy Father Pope John Paul II: Meeting with Ecclesial Movements and New Communities, May 30, 1998, https://w2.vatican.va/content/john-paul-ii/en/speeches/1998/may/documents/hf_jp-ii_spe_19980530_riflessioni.html.

the Church can equally be described as charismatic. Charisms are an essential part of the Church's inheritance from Christ because they are necessary to fulfill her mission. If the Church were simply a human institution whose purpose is just to build a better world by means of human talent, the Church would not need spiritual gifts, that is, charisms. But because the Church is also a divine institution that relies on the power and grace of God to bring about his kingdom on earth, the Holy Spirit provides spiritual gifts for this task. (Otherwise, is the Church any different than any secular social welfare group or agency, perhaps with a spiritual veneer?) St. Paul addresses this difference directly in his First Letter to the Corinthians, the letter in which he instructs the Church at great length about the charisms and their use:

> No one comprehends the thoughts of God except the Spirit of God. Now we have received not the spirit of the world, but the Spirit which is from God, that we might understand the gifts bestowed on us by God. . . . The unspiritual [or natural] man does not receive the gifts of the Spirit of God, for they are folly to him, and he is not able to understand them because they are spiritually discerned. . . . "For who has known the mind of the Lord so as to instruct him?" But we have the mind of Christ. (1 Corinthians 2:11-12, 14, 16)

Perhaps the greatest obstacle in speaking about (or using) charisms today in the Catholic Church, more than fifty years after the close of Vatican II, is that most Catholics still think of them as something reserved for a particular group, and often as something cultish and not really Catholic. If the sacraments or certain Catholic devotions and practices appear cultish and strange to someone (which they can), what do we do? We instruct people about them; we catechize the people! If charisms still seem strange and cultish to many Catholics today, either they have not been introduced or exposed to the charisms, or they have not been properly catechized about their meaning and use. The Renewal has been one place in the Church where the charisms have been encouraged, used, and explained, in response to Vatican II's teaching and God's outpouring of these gifts of the Spirit in our time. Here they no longer appear as strange, esoteric, or cultish. The Renewal has found ways to integrate charisms into normal Catholic life. This is a contribution that the Renewal has to offer to the whole Catholic Church.

As we have seen, St. Peter urges, "As each has received a gift, employ it for one another, as good stewards of God's varied grace" (1 Peter 4:10). And Vatican II's *Apostolicam Actuositatem* exhorts,

> From the reception of these charisms, even the most ordinary ones, there arises for each of the faithful the right and duty of exercising them in the Church and in the world for the good of men and the development of the Church, of exercising them in the freedom of the Holy Spirit who "breathes where he will" (John 3:8). (3)

In this chapter and the next, we will explore the meaning and proper use of some of these charisms that have come to the fore in this "charismatic" renewal. In discussing the charisms that are most characteristic of the present-day Renewal, we can distinguish between charisms predominantly used for worship or in a worship setting and those that are exercised more specifically for ministry or service.

Some charisms, notably prophecy, usually are used in a worship setting, yet their purpose is to minister to other people: to strengthen their faith or to provide insight or direction. People in the Renewal often use the term "word gifts" when they are discussing gifts normally used in worship, including the charism of prophesy. In prayer meetings, there may be an individual or a few people whose charism is discernment of spirits (see 1 Corinthians 12:10). Those who believe they have a prophecy, an exhortation, or a Scripture reading for the meeting will submit it to a designated person or group discerning these "word gifts." This is one way of following St. Paul's advice about proper order when the Christian community gathers for prayer (see 1 Corinthians 14:26-33). Let's examine some of these charisms of word and worship that have emerged in a new way and with new power in this Renewal.

Prophecy

St. Paul considered prophecy the premier charism for the Church: "Make love your aim, and earnestly desire the spiritual gifts, especially that you may prophesy" (1 Corinthians

14:1). Jesus promised that he would send the Holy Spirit to guide the Church and to reveal "things that are to come" (John 16:13); the gift of prophecy is one way this promise is fulfilled.

When we speak about prophecy as it is experienced in the Renewal, it is important to clarify what it is and what it is not. The charism of prophecy in the Renewal isn't divine (or public) revelation, as are the prophetic books of the Old Testament or the prophetic statements of Jesus or the apostles in the New Testament. This is why all prophecy after the canon of Scripture was determined must be discerned or tested, and the basic standard for discernment for Catholics is divine revelation—Sacred Scripture and Sacred Tradition. A prophecy given today might say more than what is in divine revelation, but it must never express anything opposed to divine revelation; that would be false prophecy.

So if the charism of prophecy is not public revelation, what is its purpose? It is based on the belief that God can and does continue to communicate, to speak to his people, fulfilling (in one way) Jesus' promise that he is with us always (Matthew 28:20) and demonstrating that the Holy Spirit can and will reveal things for the benefit of those gathered in worship or for the broader church community.

What does the Lord speak through this charism? Words of encouragement, direction, warning, or rebuke—whatever a particular group who is gathered in his name needs to hear. Many have noted that prophecy may not always be "fore-telling," predicting something to come, but true prophecy is always "forth-telling," expressing something God desires to communicate in a particular time and place. As St. Paul tells the Corinthians, "For you can all prophesy one by one, so that all may learn and all be encouraged" (1 Corinthians 14:31).

However, all prophecy of this kind must be discerned or tested. In his earliest preserved letter, Paul writes, "Do not quench the Spirit, do not despise prophesying, but test everything; hold fast what is good" (1 Thessalonians 5:19-21). As mentioned earlier, one way of testing or discerning charismatic prophecy is for a discerning person or persons to be designated to hear the substance of a prophetic word before the person presents it to the group. Whether or not this happens, when a person speaks a prophetic word, the people listening must discern what the Lord may be speaking. It is sometimes said that a prophetic utterance may be a word from God for a particular person present there. In any case, speaking a prophetic word is an act of faith. It is humbling when the Holy Spirit speaks through a person, and it must be remembered that no prophecy is "just God" speaking, because the word of God comes through imperfect human instruments, as many of the Old Testament prophets acknowledged. This is what St. Paul means when he says that "our knowledge is imperfect and our prophecy is imperfect; but when the perfect comes [i.e., when we see God face-to-face], the imperfect will pass away" (1 Corinthians 13:9-10). However, neither is any genuine prophecy merely a human word, as it is God who is speaking, as St. Peter attests to (2 Peter 1:21).

The charism of prophecy in the Renewal has proven to be a great gift. People *expect* that God can and does give encouragement, help, direction, and correction to individuals and groups when they turn to him in prayer. We can have expectant faith that God is with us and desires to speak to us. This is why St. Paul sees prophecy as such an important gift to the Christian community.

In the Renewal, there have been some prophecies given at major gatherings that have made an impact on the lives and perspectives of many people, even beyond those present at the time. One that is etched in my mind is a prophecy given by Ralph Martin at a massive ecumenical charismatic gathering held in Arrowhead Stadium in Kansas City, Missouri, in 1977. The prophecy repeated the refrain, "Mourn and weep, for the Body of my Son is broken." Everyone in the stadium was on their knees or prostrate, and there was weeping and lamentation for the division among Christians.

Two years earlier, at St. Peter's Basilica in Rome on Pentecost Monday, a number of prophesies were given from the high altar at the close of the Mass. Some of these prophecies spoke of difficulties and trials that would come upon the world and upon Christians but also of the dawn of a new age for God's Church and "a time of evangelization that the world has never seen." This was in May 1975, and in December 1975, Blessed Pope Paul VI issued *Evangelii Nuntiandi* [On Evangelization in the Modern World], which was one of the most powerful papal documents on evangelization ever written and which launched a "new evangelization" effort by the Catholic Church, continued by Pope St. John Paul II and subsequent popes. The prophetic word resonated even in papal teaching.

Stemming from the Renewal, there was a surge of writing on the charisms in the 1970s, much of which was written by Catholic authors.[4] However, the real difficulty most Catholics today have with recognizing the validity of the gift of prophecy and most of the other charisms in the Renewal is that they don't believe that these charisms can occur today in the same way that they did in New Testament times. In that case, it is futile to cite Sacred Scripture or the Fathers of the Church to those who have already made up their minds that these charisms cannot (or should not) be present in the Church today. Fr. Francis A. Sullivan, SJ, then professor at Rome's Gregorian University, noted in his 1982 book *Charisms and Charismatic Renewal: A Biblical and Theological Study,* that if the prophetic gifts are useful, as St. Paul judged them to be, "I see no reason to reject outright the possibility that the Holy

---

4. Protestant scholar Arnold Bittlinger had published a book, *Gifts and Graces: Commentary on 1 Corinthians, 12–14* (Grand Rapids, MI: William B. Eerdmans Publishing Co., 1968). Books by Catholic authors included Steve Clark's *Baptized in the Spirit and Spiritual Gifts* (Pecos, NM: Dove Publications, 1976), Fr. George T. Montague, SM's *The Spirit and His Gifts* (New York: Paulist Press, 1974), and Msgr. Vincent Walsh's *A Key to Charismatic Renewal in the Catholic Church* (Holland, PA: Key of David Publications, 1974; see chapter 7 on prophecy). Bruce Yocum, an early leader of the Renewal in Ann Arbor, Michigan, and one who delivered a powerful prophecy at St. Peter's on Pentecost Monday 1975, published a book, *Prophecy: Exercising the Prophetic Gifts in the Spirit in the Church Today* (Ann Arbor, MI: Servant Publications, 1976), that became a standard source of instruction on prophecy in the Renewal. More recent books on the charisms include Fr. Peter Coughlin's *Understanding the Charismatic Gifts* (Burlington, ON: Bread of Life Renewal Center, 1998) and a booklet entitled *Charisms,* ed. Sr. Mary Anne Schaenzer, SSND (Locust Grove, VA: National Service Committee of the Catholic Charismatic Renewal in the U.S., 2009).

Spirit might be giving this gift today to ordinary Christians who earnestly desire it, and ask for it, for the sake of its usefulness for the building up of their communities."[5]

More recently, Fr. Edward D. O'Connor, CSC, who was present at the beginning of the Renewal at Notre Dame, published a masterful book in 2007, pointing out that despite all the biblical teaching on prophecy and its importance in the Renewal, most people are not accustomed to seeing the gift operating:

> It seems that most of the people most of the time take what they are accustomed to as the norm. And since the life of most Christians today does not involve any conscious contact with the Spirit of God, and particularly not with any prophets, when they do encounter someone claiming to deliver a message from the Lord, they pull back with misgivings.[6]

Prophecy (as well as "speaking in tongues" and healing) violates what some jokingly call the eleventh commandment of Catholic parish life: "Don't rock the boat!" Fortunately, the Spirit of God has been at work in the Catholic Church in many ways over the past fifty years, enabling Catholics to reject this "commandment" and open us more to the Holy Spirit's new life and work in the Church.

5. Francis A. Sullivan, SJ, *Charisms and Charismatic Renewal: A Biblical and Theological Study* (Ann Arbor, MI: Servant Books, 1982), 116.

6. Fr. Edward D. O'Connor, CSC, *I Am Sending You Prophets: The Role of Apparitions in the History of the Church* (Goleta, CA: Queenship, 2007), 60–61.

Speaking in Tongues

If there is any charism that popularly characterizes and stigmatizes Catholics in this Renewal, it is speaking in tongues. Even though it is the gift most commonly mentioned in the Acts of the Apostles when people receive the Holy Spirit, today it is so foreign and strange that it causes many Catholics to write off or avoid the Renewal.

Catholic theologians and Biblical scholars in the Renewal who have examined the gift of tongues have made some observations that help to clarify the nature and proper exercise of this gift. Here are some of their conclusions that shed light on this charism.

First, speaking in tongues is not a necessary sign of being baptized in the Spirit (as classical Pentecostals hold), nor is the "goal" of the Renewal to have everyone speak in tongues. As the Malines Document stated in 1974:

> The charismatic renewal does not have as its object the introduction of all Christians into the practice of praying in tongues. It does, however, wish to call attention to the full spectrum of the gifts of the Spirit, of which tongues is one, and to open the local churches to the possibility of the full spectrum being manifested in their midst. These gifts belong to the normal, day-to-day life of the local church, and should not be looked upon as unusual or extraordinary.[7]

7. Malines Document I, 53.

St. Paul, who wrote the most about this gift in his letters, implies that this charism is a less important gift *for the Church*, because it edifies oneself and not the Church (1 Corinthians 14:4, 12, 19). Yet he also remarks, "Now I want you all to speak in tongues, but even more to prophesy" (14:5), and "I thank God that I speak in tongues more than you all" (14:18). He also says, bluntly, "Do not forbid speaking in tongues" (14:39). And yet, according to the Malines Document, speaking in tongues "does not belong to the center of the Gospel proclamation."[8] In the Gospels, it is only mentioned once, as a "sign [that] will accompany those who believe" (Mark 16:17).

Second, there are different meanings and expressions attached to speaking in tongues and several contexts in which this charism is mentioned in the New Testament.

1. In Acts 2, St. Luke wants to stress the universality of the gospel message, and so the "miracle" of the disciples' proclamation of the gospel at Pentecost is that all the foreign listeners *hear them speaking in their own native language* (cf. Acts 2:11). This is the only time in Acts or anywhere else in Scripture that the gift of tongues is described in this way.

2. Speaking in tongues as prayer, especially praise. This is the most common form of the gift of tongues in the Renewal, as the Malines Document explain, "Those outside the renewal who are attempting to evaluate the charism of tongues will

_____

8. Ibid., 52.

fail if it is not understood in the framework of prayer. It is essentially a prayer gift, enabling many using it to pray at a deeper level."[9]

In practice, prayer in tongues in the Renewal is usually either an expression of praise or of intercessory prayer, as St. Paul describes it in his Letter to the Romans:

> Likewise the Spirit helps us in our weakness; for we do not know how to pray as we ought, but the Spirit himself intercedes for us with sighs too deep for words. And he who searches the hearts of men knows what is the mind of the Spirit, because the Spirit intercedes for the saints according to the will of God. (8:26-27)

Another form of prayer in tongues is "singing in tongues," a beautiful and often melodious expression of praise and worship, which can be expressed either in personal or group worship. St. Paul refers to this form of prayer when he writes, "I will pray with the spirit and I will pray with the mind also; I will sing with the spirit and I will sing with the mind also" (1 Corinthians 14:15). St. Augustine calls singing in tongues *jubilatio* (jubilation) and describes it in a commentary on Psalm 32:

> Take the case of people singing while harvesting in the fields or in the vineyards or when any other strenuous work is in progress. Although they begin by giving expression to their

---

9. Ibid.

happiness in sung words, yet shortly there is a change. As if so happy that words can no longer express what they feel, they discard the restricting syllables. They burst out into a simple sound of joy, of jubilation. Such a cry of joy is a sound signifying that the heart is bringing to birth what it cannot utter in words.

Now, who is more worthy of such a cry of jubilation than God himself, whom all words fail to describe? If words will not serve, and yet you must not remain silent, what else can you do but cry out for joy? Your heart must rejoice beyond words, soaring into an immensity of gladness, unrestrained by syllabic bonds. *Sing to him with songs of joy.*[10]

The contrast between praying with the "mind" and with the "spirit" has led most commentators to describe speaking in tongues as a kind of "nonconceptual" prayer. This is confirmed by St. Paul's description in Romans 8:26, when he says that we do not "*know* how to pray as we ought" (my emphasis), but the Spirit prays within us with "inexpressible groanings" or "sighs too deep for words."

3. Speaking in tongues as conveying a prophetic message. This is a topic that St. Paul is primarily concerned with addressing in 1 Corinthians 14: keeping good order in a prayer gathering. A prophetic word could be spoken either in the language of the congregation or in a "tongue." Paul rightly insists that one person speak at a time so that all may be heard and that

10. Augustine, *Psalm 32.1.8* (CCL 38:253–54).

if there is a message or prophecy in a "tongue," then an interpretation is necessary so that all will understand what God
is saying prophetically (14:13, 27).

Fr. George Montague, SM, a prominent expert on St. Paul,
remarks,

> While, according to Paul, the primary function of tongues is
> to commune with God rather than with men, for the build-
> ing up of oneself (1 Corinthians 14:2, 4), it is also true that
> he knows of a "message in tongues" spoken out in the assem-
> bly, requiring interpretation (14:5, 13). This suggests that the
> rhythm of pre-conceptual prayer shared openly by one mem-
> ber of the assembly and followed by a "conceptualizing" of
> the experience by another [i.e., the interpretation] is part of
> the dynamic by which the community is built up (14:5). It is
> something therefore which the members of the community
> do for one another, as is the purpose of all the gifts (14:26).[11]

4. "Praying in tongues" as a known language. Most scholars agree that most often prayer in tongues is not an actual
   human language but is "nonconceptual." However, there
   have been instances when someone's speaking in tongues
   has been identified as a known human language.

---

11. Montague, *The Spirit and His Gifts*, 29.

A priest who was my spiritual director at Notre Dame, a scholarly professor, told me that one thing that convinced him of the authenticity of the Renewal was when he attended a prayer meeting and overheard a young woman praying the Hail Mary in Greek. When he asked her later whether she knew Greek, she gave him a puzzled look and said she was just praying in tongues.

For those who wonder why praying in tongues seemed to have disappeared for centuries before reemerging in the Renewal, a fascinating study by Deacon Eddie Ensley, PhD, entitled *Sounds of Wonder: 20 Centuries of Praying in Tongues and Lively Worship in the Catholic Tradition,* has recently been updated and republished. Ensley presents a convincing case that this gift never disappeared but rather remained present in the lives of Catholic saints and mystics and even found liturgical expression.

However, we are privileged today that this anointed form of prophecy and prayer is, through the Renewal, not just for mystics and saints, but is blessing many ordinary Christians with a powerful way of praising and worshipping God and building up individuals and communities in faith.

Chapter 4

Charisms of Ministry and Service

In his First Letter to the Corinthians, St. Paul lists the various ministries in the body of Christ, the Church, which flow from the charisms of ministry and service given by the Holy Spirit. Even though he doesn't say he is listing these charisms in a chronological or hierarchical order, it is noteworthy that Paul ranks the first three:

> Now you are the body of Christ and individually members of it. And God has appointed in the church first apostles, second prophets, third teachers, then workers of miracles, then healers, helpers, administrators, speakers in various kinds of tongues. (1 Corinthians 12:27-28)

After apostles, the Church relies on prophets and teachers, "ministers of the word," to guide and instruct her, as we saw in the last chapter. Paul continues his list without ranking them, starting with "workers of miracles"—certainly an extraordinary charism, but not unknown either in the early Church or today. Next on his list are "healers, helpers, administrators": the charisms of ministry and service and the basis of this chapter.

These are charisms that provide practical service to the Church and to those outside of her, rather than instruction or teaching. They enable and equip members of the body of Christ, even nonordained members, to carry out various spiritual and practical services to the Church and to the world through the power of the Holy Spirit, who gives these charisms freely, as he wills (see 1 Corinthians 12:11).

In addition to the charism of healing, we will also discuss the related charism of deliverance from evil spirits, both of which are commanded and commissioned by Jesus himself. In Matthew 10:8, Jesus instructed his disciples, "Heal the sick, raise the dead, cleanse lepers, cast out demons. You received without pay, give without pay." Mark 6:13 notes, "And they cast out many demons, and anointed with oil many that were sick and healed them."

The Gift of Healing

This charism is familiar to many Catholics, but often it is identified with particular saints who had gifts or ministries of healing or with places where many physical healings have occurred, such as Lourdes. Perhaps it is not necessary to explain what the Renewal means by "healing," but it is important to ask why there has been a greater focus on healing and a surprising number of Catholics with healing ministries in this Renewal.

The most important reason is the abundant grace and mercy of God, for God alone is the one who heals people "miraculously." The other reason, equally important, is the expectant faith that the Renewal encourages. More Catholics have come to believe that God desires many people to receive healing through prayer.

However, there are concerns about how this type of "charismatic" healing is to be approached and understood. Early on, the Malines Document gave a balanced appraisal of healing in the Renewal. It noted that "one of the tasks of the renewal is to provide models for exercising the ministry of healing both within a sacramental context and outside." It warned against an "exclusive preoccupation with physical healing," noting that interior healing should also be an important part of a healing ministry. Also to be avoided are "public and printed claims of healing without reasonable medical verification." Furthermore, the document stressed that healing as a charism should not be placed in opposition to medical care.[1]

Sacraments of Healing

Some have the impression that the Renewal only focuses on prayer for healing at prayer meetings. In the early 1970s, some leaders in the Renewal observed that many Catholics were not going to confession regularly and still saw the Sacrament of the Anointing of the Sick (which was given this new name at the Second Vatican Council) as a sacrament for people who were in imminent danger of death—Extreme Unction.

One of the best-selling books from the early days of the Renewal was *The Power in Penance: Confession and the Holy Spirit* by Fr. Michael Scanlan, TOR, then rector of St. Francis Seminary in Loretto, Pennsylvania. The book, which was translated into many languages, describes how natural and

---

1. Malines Document I, 57.

appropriate it is to pray for healing, deliverance, and strengthening of faith in administering this healing sacrament, with a "laying on of hands" by the priest.[2]

Fr. Scanlan had "stumbled" into a ministry of healing and had himself been healed of severe allergies at a healing service led by Kathryn Kuhlman in Pittsburgh. "A key element in healing is faith," he writes. "Healing is almost always associated with *someone's* faith—the faith of the sick person; the faith of the minister; the faith of the assembly."[3]

On many occasions at summer conferences at Franciscan University of Steubenville, people were healed when Fr. Ed McDonough, a priest with a healing ministry, simply processed through the aisles with the Blessed Sacrament, sometimes sprinkling holy water as he went. Healing may be brought about by the presence of Jesus in the sacraments (such as the Eucharist) and in sacramentals (e.g., holy water, blessed oil, or blessed salt), but Fr. Scanlan insists that the most important factor is faith, and that means first asking God what he wants you to pray for.

Do not be afraid to hear the Lord telling you that he wants someone to be healed—now. I think the Lord often offers

---

2. Michael Scanlan, TOR, *The Power in Penance: Confession and the Holy Spirit* (Notre Dame, IN: Ave Maria Press, 1972). On God's power present in all the sacraments of the Church, see also his book with Ann Therese Shields, *And Their Eyes Were Opened: Discovering Jesus in the Sacraments* (Ann Arbor, MI: Servant Books, 1976).

3. Michael Scanlan, TOR, with James Manney, *Let the Fire Fall*, 2nd Edition (Steubenville, OH: Franciscan University Press, 1997), 134.

us a gift of faith, and we decline it because we are afraid to step out and pray with complete confidence. . . .

The Lord has given special healing ministries to certain individuals, but he also wants every Christian to pray for healing regularly and routinely.[4]

Most Catholics, even many Catholics in the Renewal today, do not pray for healing "regularly and routinely." However, one of the fruits of the Renewal is that "healing" Masses—Masses that incorporate prayers for healing, praying over people, or even the Sacrament of the Anointing of the Sick—and other types of healing services or ministries have become much more common in the Catholic Church.

Prominent Catholic Healing Ministries

In the early days of the Renewal, the person most visibly identified with the healing ministry was Francis MacNutt (at that time a Dominican priest). This articulate, educated, white-robed ambassador of the healing gifts and ministry made the charism of healing known through his healing ministry and his writings, beginning with his book *Healing*.[5] Dr. MacNutt and his wife, Judith, continue to minister through their Christian

---

4. Ibid., 136, 137.

5. Francis MacNutt, *Healing* (Notre Dame, IN: Ave Maria Press, 1974). He also wrote *The Power to Heal* (Notre Dame, IN: Ave Maria Press, 1979) and *The Practice of Healing Prayer: A How-To Guide for Catholics* (Frederick, MD: The Word Among Us Press, 2010).

Healing Ministries in Jacksonville, Florida. More recently, other healing ministries have continued to emerge and grow throughout the world under the direction of people such as English lay Catholic Damian Stayne, Bob Canton, and others.

To give guidance and direction to Catholics for the charisms of healing, International Catholic Charismatic Renewal Services (ICCRS) sponsored a colloquium on healing in Rome in November 2001 with the support of the Pontifical Council for the Laity. Talks on the topic of healing were presented by bishops and members of important Vatican congregations, among other contributors. The final lecture, entitled "Healing in the Catholic Charismatic Renewal," was given by Bishop Albert-Marie de Monléon, OP, of Meaux, France, who, as a priest, was involved in the Renewal in France from its earliest days. In this talk, he mentioned three things that characterize healing in the Renewal that are distinctive and sometimes different from the traditional or historical ideas of healing in the Catholic Church.

1. "Healings are not primarily linked to the presence of relics or places of pilgrimage. They take place much more within the context of evangelization and the celebration of the sacraments, or in prayer meetings, or even in specific meetings directed and organized by people who are said to be persons possessing a 'charism of healing.'"

2. Healings "are closely linked to evangelization, to the proclamation of the Gospel, and attraction to the Kingdom."

3. "The way in which healings are generally experienced in the Renewal is as a 'sign' of the compassion of God welcomed in joy and thanksgiving, rather than as 'wonders' or miracles, whose medically inexplicable and apologetically indisputable character is emphasized."[6]

Bishop de Monléon went on to explain that, as much as possible, healing in the Catholic Charismatic Renewal is done either within a sacramental framework or by focusing on the integration of prayer for healing with the sacramental life, including baptism, reconciliation, and the Eucharist.

In the United States, praying over people for healing often is done after a Mass with a healing theme, which is also an attempt to make the charism of healing more known and available in the life of the broader Church. This helps to serve and attract Catholics who would not go to a prayer meeting or healing service but would come to a Mass that includes prayer for healing.

It should also be noted that, whatever the context may be, many healings do occur in the Renewal, and this, I believe, is true because of the expectant faith that God can and does heal. Jesus himself, on a number of occasions, stressed the important role of faith when people were healed. If healings in the Renewal are more frequent, said de Monléon in his presentation, "It is not because they are the privilege of the 'Charismatics' but

6. Albert-Marie de Monléon, OP, "Healing in the Catholic Charismatic Renewal," in *Prayer for Healing* (Rome, Italy: International Catholic Charismatic Renewal Services, 2003), 205–206.

simply because they are more recognized, more readily welcomed, and are considered to form part of the heritage of the Church, of normal Christian life." He also emphasized that healings "should never be considered as isolated, individual events, but they are accompanied by a far-reaching change (*metanoia*) in the life of the people who are healed."[7]

Deliverance from Evil Spirits

Deliverance from evil spirits may be seen as one of the more controversial aspects of the Renewal, but that is largely due to a general skepticism in our time and culture about the reality of the demonic or of evil spirits, even about the existence of Satan. It may be true that some problems that were attributed to evil spirits and demonic forces in times past may have had natural, medical, or psychological causes. And it is a fact that any mention of the demonic today conjures up images of the witch hunts in Salem or of hyper-dramatic movies like *The Exorcist*.

These factors prejudice most Catholics against anything having to do with evil spirits except for formal prayers of exorcism in the liturgy, rites of sacraments, or perhaps the office of exorcist in the Church. It is somewhat ironic in this regard that one of the most well-known and often-used prayers among Catholics is Pope Leo XIII's prayer to St. Michael, who is invoked to "defend us in battle and be our protection against the wickedness and snares of the devil." For most Catholics, this prayer covers any concern we might have about the devil.

---

7. Ibid., 209.

However, one result of the Renewal is that in calling people to open up more to God, in particular to God the Holy Spirit, sometimes the existence of seemingly inexplicable obstacles to God's Spirit working in the lives of people becomes more apparent. In the early days of the Renewal, Catholics became familiar with some writings of other Christians that addressed deliverance from evil spirits, such as Anglican Michael Harper's book *Spiritual Warfare* (Plainfield, NJ: Logos International, 1970). Notably, Pope Paul VI also called attention to the reality and nefarious activity of Satan in an audience given on November 15, 1972:

> What are the greatest needs of the Church today? Do not let our answer surprise you as being simplistic or even superstitious and unreal: one of the greatest needs is defense from that evil which is called the Devil. . . . So we know that this dark and disturbing spirit really exists, and that he still acts with treacherous cunning; he is the secret enemy that sows errors and misfortunes in human history.[8]

Three years later, the Sacred Congregation of the Doctrine of the Faith issued a document, "Christian Faith and

---

8. Paul VI, General Audience, November 15, 1972, https://w2.vatican.va/content/paul-vi/it/audiences/1972/documents/hf_p-vi_aud_19721115.html.

Demonology," that confirmed the reality of Satan and the danger of his activity against the human race.[9]

Of course, some Catholics may be familiar with C. S. Lewis' *Screwtape Letters,* which deftly introduces one to the possibility of demonic sources of temptation and the idea that Satan might actually have a strategy against individuals that is actively opposing God's grace and plan for their lives.

These sources confirmed what modern Catholics were beginning to doubt but which Catholics in the Renewal knew was true from the Bible, Tradition, and sometimes their own experience: that Satan and evils spirits are real and active in the world and in the lives of ordinary people today. In the Renewal, there were people who, once they started following the Lord more consciously, began to find areas of bondage in their lives. There were also those who had a seemingly irrational resistance to asking for or receiving prayer.

To determine whether these things were the work of evil spirits or the result of other causes, the charism of discernment of spirits was required (see 1 Corinthians 12:10). And if it appeared that there was some spiritual influence causing the problem, prayer for deliverance from evil spirits could be undertaken. In some Catholic prayer groups, it was common to include a simple prayer rebuking Satan and evil spirits for those seeking either baptism in the Holy Spirit or other prayer ministry. This ministry of deliverance and conscious "spiritual

---

9. The Sacred Congregation for the Doctrine of the Faith, "Christian Faith and Demonology," June 26, 1975, http://www.vatican.va/roman_curia/congregations/cfaith/documents/rc_con_cfaith_doc_19750626_fede-cristiana-demonologia_en.html.

warfare" against Satan and evil spirits was not universal in the Renewal (as were baptism in the Spirit and the gifts of prophecy, speaking in tongues, or even healing), but it is a part of the history of the Renewal.

In 1980 Fr. Michael Scanlan, TOR, then president of Franciscan University of Steubenville, coauthored a book entitled *Deliverance from Evil Spirits: A Weapon for Spiritual Warfare*.[10] The book had an *imprimatur* and *nihil obstat* through Fr. Scanlan's religious community, and his stature as a college president likely made the idea of a deliverance ministry more acceptable to Catholics who would understandably be somewhat skeptical about this focus on Satan and evil spirits.

This topic was not just an American concern. It was addressed in Europe by another Malines consultation, held again under the leadership of Cardinal Leon-Joseph Suenens, which led to the publication of Malines Document IV, entitled *Renewal and the Power of Darkness*.[11]

It is notable that the foreword to this book was written in 1982 by Cardinal Joseph Ratzinger, then prefect of the Sacred Congregation of the Doctrine of the Faith, who later became Pope Benedict XVI. He writes,

---

10. Michael Scanlan, TOR, and Randall J. Cirner, *Deliverance from Evil Spirits: A Weapon for Spiritual Warfare* (Ann Arbor, MI: Servant Books, 1980).

11. Cardinal Leon-Joseph Suenens, *Renewal and the Powers of Darkness*, Malines IV (U.S. publisher: Ann Arbor, MI: Servant Books, 1983).

While a rationalist and reductionist theology is explaining away the Devil and the world of evil spirits as a mere label for everything that threatens man in his subjectivity, a new, concrete awareness of the Powers of Evil and their cunning, which threaten man, is growing in the context of the Renewal.

This awareness has given rise to a "prayer of deliverance from the Devil" which has developed to the point of resembling a rite of exorcism and of becoming, today, an integral part of the life of some charismatic groups.

While cautioning that wisdom and moderation are needed, Ratzinger urged readers to study the practical directives offered by Cardinal Suenens. Noting that Cardinal Suenens' work "is as important for the Renewal movement as for the whole Church," he adds,

I also urge [Christians] to pay special attention to the Cardinal's double plea, which deserves the greatest consideration: on the one hand, his appeal to those responsible for the ecclesial ministry—from parish priests to bishops—not to let the Renewal pass them by but to welcome it fully; and on the other, his appeal to the members of the Renewal to cherish and maintain their link with the whole Church and with the charisms of her pastors.

Ratzinger concludes, "As Prefect of the Congregation for the Doctrine of the Faith, I warmly welcome this work by

Cardinal Suenens: it is an important contribution to the blossoming of the spiritual life in today's Church."[12]

This affirmation by the Church's chief doctrinal authority at the time demonstrates the timelessness and the importance of the Renewal's response to the activity of Satan and evil spirits and the need to employ charisms of discernment and prayer against the activity of evil in Catholic ministry. Cardinal Ratzinger considered this a contribution of the Renewal to the entire Church.

Since that time, other books by leaders from the Catholic Renewal have appeared, including one by Neal Lozano called *Unbound: A Practical Guide to Deliverance,* which has been used extensively in parishes and dioceses.[13]

The Charism of Discernment/Guidance

A final charism of ministry and service that has emerged in the Renewal is the charism of guidance for people's lives. This is an important aspect of spiritual direction and is also a practical charism that God gives to some ordinary laypeople as well. It is not surprising that, in a movement that emphasizes the need for and the possibility of "hearing the Lord" through prayer and prophecy, such a charism would be present in order to know God's will and to follow it.

---

12. Ibid., ix–xi.

13. Neal Lozano, *Unbound: A Practical Guide to Deliverance* (Grand Rapids, MI: Baker/Chosen Books, 2003).

Many books have been written on the topic, with the authors also referencing and drawing from the great Catholic classics of discernment such as the principles formed by St. Ignatius of Loyola, founder of the Society of Jesus, in his *Spiritual Exercises*.[14]

The Renewal also has produced centers where people are being trained in spiritual direction based on Catholic tradition and sound Catholic theology but with a charismatic emphasis, since it is the Holy Spirit who is the source of all authentic spiritual direction and guidance. The Cenacle of Our Lady of Divine Providence in Clearwater, Florida, has such a program for the training and certification of spiritual directors; it is underwritten and supported by the theology department of Franciscan University of Steubenville.

The charism of guidance and discernment for making decisions is often carried out in the Renewal in the context of prayer groups or, more frequently, in covenant communities. The emergence of these social expressions and forms of the Renewal will be the subject of the next chapter.

---

14. Some books published on this topic by people involved in the Renewal include Steve Clark, *Knowing God's Will* (Ann Arbor, MI: Servant Books, 1974); Robert Faricy, SJ, *Seeking Jesus in Contemplation and Discernment* (Westminster, MD: Christian Classics, 1983); John J. Boucher, *Is Talking to God a Long-Distance Call? How to Hear and Understand God's Voice* (Ann Arbor, MI: Servant Books, 1990); Susan Muto and Adrian van Kaam, *Divine Guidance: Seeking to Find and Follow the Will of God* (Ann Arbor, MI: Servant Books, 1994); and Michael Scanlan, TOR, with James Manney, *What Does God Want? A Practical Guide to Making Decisions* (Huntington, IN: Our Sunday Visitor Press, 1996).

Chapter 5

Community

The Importance of Spiritual Support and Fellowship

Koinonia is the Greek word used in the New Testament for communion, community, or fellowship. One unmistakable work of the Holy Spirit in the Catholic Charismatic Renewal is an awakening to the importance of *koinonia*. If being baptized in the Spirit identifies a person as being part of the Renewal, one could conclude that this movement is just a particular spirituality focused on a deeper relationship with God in the Holy Spirit and on spiritual gifts or charisms. Though these undoubtedly are marks of the Renewal, it also has a profound social or communal dimension.

Most Catholics who have been baptized in the Spirit received this grace in a communal context, with others present praying for them and over them with the laying on of hands. After that experience, they don't normally just go off and live this grace on their own; they usually participate, at least for a time, in a prayer group or community. Christian participation in some form of communal life is a pattern that began on Pentecost with the first great outpouring of the Spirit on Jesus' followers. This event was accompanied by God pouring out an abundance of charisms, primarily to build up the Church, the body of Christ. As Fr. Francis Martin put it, the charisms are "communally conceived"—they are gifts for the body of Christ, the community of the Church, and they also enable the Church to carry out her mission and ministry to others, as we discussed in the previous two chapters of this book. How often in these groups do we hear this Scripture passage from the Letter to the Hebrews: "Let us consider how to stir up one another to love and good works, not neglecting to meet together, as is the habit of some, but encouraging one another, and all the more as you see the Day drawing near" (10:24-25)?

In a charismatic prayer group or community, the charisms are used to worship God as a community or to serve others. Worship might include praying or singing in tongues and listening to the Lord, either silently or through a prophetic word, an exhortation, or a reading from Sacred Scripture or another inspirational source. Serving might be directed toward those within the group or those outside through some outreach.

Forms of Community or Fellowship

When the Renewal began, those baptized in the Spirit naturally desired to meet together to pray and to support one another in following the Lord, in growing spiritually, and in learning more about God and the Christian life. Through the Renewal, God sparked a hunger for reading Scripture and spiritual books. And yet the first groups that emerged from the Renewal were not Bible studies or other study groups but prayer groups where people could worship God freely in the Spirit. Yes, these prayer groups sometimes gave rise to Bible studies or other study groups, but the focus was on prayer, which included hearing the Lord's word through Scripture, prophecy, exhortation, and sometimes teachings on various topics. People drawn together to pray also built relationships and often wanted to find ways to support each other in daily life. One of the works and signs of the Holy Spirit's presence is unity based on love, as we see in the gatherings of Christ's followers after Pentecost. Through the grace of the Renewal, many Catholics who had previously understood the Church primarily as a place you go to receive the sacraments or for certain events (a parish picnic; holy hour; various men's, women's, or youth groups) began to understand their need for personal spiritual support to grow in their renewed life in Christ and in God's call to serve and support others. They began to experience firsthand the words of Psalm 133:1: "Behold, how good and pleasant it is when brethren dwell in unity" and of Acts 4:32: "Now the company of those who believed were of one heart and soul."

It was also natural that they were drawn to associate in this way with those who shared a similar experience of renewal by being baptized in the Spirit. They had come to understand what it means that Jesus truly is Lord of their lives and of all things, and they wanted to live the teachings of Jesus and the Church more fully and faithfully. The joy and the blessing of coming together to praise God, to be strengthened by his word, and to share in this fellowship were the magnets that drew people to charismatic prayer groups. (And, of course, many came initially just to see what was happening in these meetings.)

This desire of those in the Renewal to meet together has taken different forms, and the first ones to emerge were prayer groups and covenant communities. Each of these forms requires careful attention if one is to understand how the Renewal has unfolded in its first fifty years. Because of their powerful influence on the life and direction of the Renewal almost from their beginnings, let's first consider the emergence and life of covenant communities in the Renewal.

Covenant Communities in the Renewal

To understand why covenant communities emerged, recall the statement in the *Life in the Spirit Seminar Team Manual* that baptism in the Holy Spirit was not to be viewed as just an experience of God but as an opportunity and an invitation from God to enter into a fully committed Christian life—a life of Christian discipleship. The group that developed this team manual was led by Ralph Martin and Steve Clark, who had both moved from the Michigan State University Catholic student center in Lansing to a similar position at the Newman Center at the University of Michigan in Ann Arbor. Under their leadership, many members who attended the prayer meeting at the Newman Center and who desired a deeper, more formal commitment to each other to grow in the Christian life made a covenant with one another as a pledge of mutual support.

Of course, the idea of "covenant" has a rich scriptural background, which was understood as something God had initiated to call individuals together to be his own people in a special way. Those who began this community in Ann Arbor, Michigan, similarly believed that God was inviting them to commit themselves to each other in order to grow in their lives as Christians and to carry out God's will for them, whatever that might be. They sought God's will together through prayer, prophecy, and other charisms. As they joined together as a community, they believed God gave them a name through prophecy and various Scripture passages: the Word of God. This community began in the fall of 1967.

Of course, the most important question and concern was whether a "covenant community" was a new "church" (or "sect," in sociological terms). Did it replace or supersede membership in an established Christian church or denomination? It should be noted that the Word of God was ecumenical in its origin, though heavily Catholic in membership and leadership. The covenant made clear that this commitment did not replace or exclude membership in an established ecclesial body (such as the Catholic Church), and it encouraged active church membership. The Word of God claimed no doctrinal authority other than following the commonly acknowledged authority of the Bible. This is important, because it became the standard approach in this matter for nearly all the other covenant communities that later emerged in the Renewal. Communities that were entirely Catholic also followed Catholic teaching in their common life.

Before too long, covenant communities sprang up all over the country. Some of these, like the Word of God, were ecumenical in membership; others were entirely Catholic. Members of the

Word of God belonged to local churches or to a "free church fellowship," called Emmaus, for community members pastored by others in the community. In South Bend, the People of Praise was established as an ecumenical covenant community led by Kevin Ranaghan and Paul DeCelles, although they kept close ties with the Catholic Church and were both ordained permanent deacons. They also established a training program for deacons in South Bend approved by the diocese, the Apostolic Institute. On the Notre Dame campus, a community composed predominantly of students and entirely Catholic in membership, called True House, was formed under the leadership of Jim Byrne and Peter Edwards, with Fr. Edward D. O'Connor, CSC, as primary spiritual director and mentor. (I was a member of True House from the spring of 1970 until the fall of 1974, when I left for graduate school.) A House of Prayer in New Jersey evolved into a covenant community, the People of Hope, under the leadership of Fr. Jim Ferry. Other communities around the country also formed, often mentored by or modeled upon these first charismatic covenant communities.

Due to strong leadership and highly committed members, the Word of God, the People of Praise, and True House had tremendous influence on the direction of the Renewal in its early years. Some of the specific means of this influence included:

- An annual leaders' conference held in Ann Arbor.

- *New Covenant*, a magazine that was a primary vehicle of teaching and communication in the Renewal in the U.S. It was published in Ann Arbor with Ralph Martin as its first editor, succeeded by Dr. Bert Ghezzi.

- Word of Life Publications, also located in Ann Arbor, which distributed tapes and books and eventually became Servant Publications.

- *Pastoral Renewal*, an ecumenical, pastoral newsletter produced and published in Ann Arbor beginning in July 1976, whose editors also hosted conferences on various themes related to the Renewal and to Christian life in modern culture.

- The Communication Center in South Bend, which produced a directory for Catholic charismatic prayer groups and communities and distributed publications on the Renewal, especially those published by Charismatic Renewal Services, Inc., also in South Bend/Notre Dame.

- Annual national and international conferences on the Catholic Charismatic Renewal, organized and run by the True House Community from 1970–1974 and thereafter by the People of Praise. These were known popularly as the "Notre Dame conferences."

- Strong representation on the National Service Committee (USA), formed in 1970 to provide direction and service to the Renewal in the United States.[1]

In addition, Cardinal Leon-Joseph Suenens of Belgium, hoping both to keep the Renewal "in the heart of the Church" and to bring the rich fruits of the Renewal to the broader Catholic Church, invited Ralph Martin and Steve Clark to work with him in Brussels, Belgium. Since at that time Martin was director of a small, fledgling office serving the international Renewal, the International Communications Office moved with him, as well as other members of the Word of God community. In Belgium, a covenant community called Jerusalem emerged out of a prayer group they started, and it still exists today. Martin and Clark maintained close communication with Cardinal Suenens, who celebrated a weekly Mass for them and others at which the charisms were manifested, just as they were in the Mass that the cardinal had celebrated for the entire Renewal at St. Peter's Basilica on Pentecost Monday 1975. Cardinal Suenens became the episcopal advisor for the International Communications Office.

---

1. The initial (1970) National Service Committee (NSC) included Jim Byrne, Fr. Edward O'Connor, CSC, Ralph Martin, Kevin Ranaghan, Steve Clark, Bert Ghezzi, and Fr. George Kosicki, CSB (who had been at Notre Dame). In 1973 Paul DeCelles of the People of Praise was added, as well as the first episcopal member, Bishop Joseph McKinney of Grand Rapids, Michigan. By 1976, 63 percent of NSC members were clergy, and by 1978 only Kevin Ranaghan remained on the NSC from the original group.

A gathering of international leaders in 1977 led to greater clarity about the office's function. An advisory board was formed, and the name was changed to the International Catholic Charismatic Renewal Office. In 1980, the office moved to Rome under the direction of Fr. Thomas Forrest, CSSR. A strong relationship was built with the Pontifical Council for the Laity, and a formal relationship with Rome was recognized in 1993, along with another name change: the International Catholic Charismatic Renewal Services (ICCRS).

It is hard to overstate the influence these covenant communities and their leadership had on the direction of the Renewal, especially in keeping it firmly within the Catholic Church and loyal to the pope and the bishops. This was a tumultuous time in the Catholic Church, during which many Catholic theologians, laypeople, and even priests and bishops were calling into question the Church's authority and basic Catholic teaching, especially in the area of morality. The key leaders in the Renewal in South Bend, Ann Arbor, and elsewhere, many of them well-educated laypeople, were rock solid in their theology and loyalty to the Catholic Church. This diffused some of the misgivings that bishops and others had about this "Pentecostal phenomenon" in the Catholic Church. (The next chapter will in turn discuss the response of the pope and bishops to the Renewal.) As an example, soon after his return to the United States, Ralph Martin published *A Crisis of Truth*, which exposed the damaging confusion caused by false theology and poor pastoral practice that was rampant in the Catholic Church. Other Catholics who were considered more "traditional" were saying the same thing. This is another way in which the Renewal was a prophetic voice in the Church and the world—calling attention to the ways that Christian values were being eroded and Christian truth compromised in our society at large and even within the Church. Covenant communities sought to help their members to live daily according to the principles found in Sacred Scripture, proclaiming those principles to others through the way of life that is embodied in their covenants and community teaching.

For those who belonged to these communities (including my wife and me), it is amazing to recall the zeal and desire to serve the Lord that filled us and the joy that this brought even though it required many sacrifices. Sacred Scripture came alive even more because we were striving to live it out daily. We often could understand what Jesus and the authors of Scripture were talking about by virtue of our own experience as disciples of Christ living in community.

Sometimes it is said that there was tension or even conflict between those in the Renewal who belonged to a covenant community and those in prayer groups. It is true that within the Renewal, there were different callings and different visions and that those in covenant community were tempted to think (because of the richness of their community experience) that this is how *everyone* in the Renewal and in the Church should be living or aspiring to live. (Sadly, sometimes in pride or narrow-mindedness, we succumbed to that temptation.) Yet many of those in covenant communities served those in the broader Renewal through the ministries or outreaches of the communities. As mentioned earlier, teaching resources such as the Life in the Spirit Seminar manuals, *New Covenant* magazine, *Pastoral Renewal,* and many books helpful to those in the Renewal were produced by or under the auspices of covenant communities and their ministries. Much of the wonderful worship music enjoyed by people in the Renewal was composed by members of covenant communities and produced and distributed by them. Bible studies and aids for daily Scripture reading abounded. Thousands of people annually attended conferences that were organized and staffed largely by members of covenant communities.[2]

Besides the Notre Dame conferences, other major Catholic charismatic conferences were organized in Atlantic City, in the football stadium now known as MetLife Stadium in the Meadowlands, and at Shea Stadium by the People of Hope community and other prayer groups in the vicinity. And, of course, the 1975 international charismatic conference held on the grounds of the catacombs in Rome and at St. Peter's Basilica was staffed by the People of Praise, the Word of God, and members of the Renewal in France and Italy (especially Rome).

By the late 1970s, the time of these massive charismatic conferences had passed. They were succeeded by smaller conferences around the country, including some run by covenant

---

2. This was one of my contributions as coordinator/administrator of the 1973 and 1974 International Charismatic Conferences at Notre Dame, attended by 22,000 and 25,000 people, respectively. I also had the opportunity to assist with regional charismatic conferences held in Augusta, Georgia; Minneapolis, Minnesota; San Diego, California; and Montreal, Canada, in 1973 and 1974 and in Toronto, Canada, in 1976.

communities, such as the Steubenville summer conferences that were first administered and served by members of the Servants of Christ the King community in Steubenville, Ohio. Thousands of peoples' lives were touched by the Holy Spirit through attending these conferences, for which covenant communities often were primarily responsible, and which were powerful manifestations of the graces that were coming to the Church through the Renewal.[3]

Within the first few years of the Renewal, many of these covenant communities were established in different parts of the United States, a number of them following the model of the Word of God and the People of Praise. Some were "branches" of these communities.[4] In addition, there were other covenant

---

3. These included the Bible institute, priests and deacons conference, youth conference, charismatic conference, sisters conference, and the F.I.R.E. rallies—an acronym for Faith, Intercession, Repentance, Evangelization, preached initially by Fr. John Bertolucci, Ralph Martin, Sr. Ann Shields, and Fr. Michael Scanlan, TOR.

4. Though not a comprehensive list, the early covenant communities in the United States included People of H.O.P.E. (House of Prayer Experience), Newark, New Jersey; Ignatius House/Community of God's Love, Rutherford, New Jersey; Lamb of God, Baltimore, Maryland; Mother of God, Potomac/Gaithersburg, Maryland; Alleluia Community, Augusta, Georgia; Community of God's Love, Steubenville, Ohio; Bread of Life, Akron, Ohio; New Jerusalem, Cincinnati, Ohio; Work of Christ, Lansing, Michigan; Servants of the Light/Lord, Minneapolis, Minnesota; Jesus the King, New Orleans, Louisiana; Community of God's Delight, Dallas, Texas; People of Joy, Phoenix, Arizona; City of the Angels, Los Angeles, California; St. John the Baptist Community, San Francisco, California; and Southern California Renewal Communities (SCRC), led for many years by Fr. Ralph Tichenor, SJ.

communities in the 1970s, both large and small, springing up around the world.[5]

Some of these communities took different approaches to aspects of their community life than the first covenant communities. For example, many of the first covenant communities had exclusively male overall leadership, which contrasted with prayer groups, which were often led by women or had women in their core leadership team. The Mother of God covenant community in Gaithersburg, Maryland, included women, Edith DiFato and Judith Tydings, in overall leadership. These covenant communities, regardless of their structure, were significant in raising up lay leaders and providing a viable model of Christian life in a society that was becoming more secular and in which Christianity was (and is) increasingly under attack and in decline. The vitality of the covenant communities and their stable, biblically based way of life were supportive to many in the Renewal and often a sign of hope and a witness to those around them—as could be seen in the rapid growth and multiplication of these communities, especially in the 1970s.

The Pattern and Vision of Covenant Communities

Where did the idea of "covenant" community come from? Fr. Robert Wild, a priest of Madonna House, wrote,

5. These included *Nueva Vida Comunidad* (New Life Community), *Aguas Buenas*, Puerto Rico; *La Ciudad de Dios* (The City of God), Managua, Nicaragua; *Ligayu ng Panginoon* (The Joy of the Lord), Manila, Philippines; Emmanuel Community, Brisbane, Australia; and the People of God, Beirut, Lebanon, to name a few.

The Roman Catholic Church has a genius for many things. One of them is its instinct to form communities. Did you ever stop to consider that the phenomenon of having religious communities on any large scale is almost exclusively a Catholic genius? The same pattern is happening again in the Catholic charismatic renewal.[6]

Fr. Wild quotes Dr. Vinson Synan, a leading authority from the Pentecostal/Holiness tradition, who noted that this strong sense of community in the Catholic Renewal was something not seen in his own Pentecostal tradition: "We are rejoicing, but we are amazed."[7] When critics of covenant community asked two of its early architects, Steve Clark and Ralph Martin, where they got their ideas and principles, Clark referred to Scripture, early Christian writings, and, in particular, the Long Rules of St. Basil and the Rule of St. Benedict. Martin mentioned the examples of the Benedictines and the Jesuits.

However, Clark, who wrote most extensively on the rationale for covenant communities, was influenced more by sound reasonable principles than by examples. Citing a 1969 book by a Belgian priest, Fr. Max Delespesse, Clark said that Delespesse's

---

6. Robert Wild, *Enthusiasm in the Spirit* (Notre Dame, IN: Ave Maria Press, 1975), 129.

7. Ibid.

approach was "remarkably similar" to his own.[8] In the introduction to his book, Delespesse wrote,

> The solution to all the problems we face today, war, hun-
> ger, overpopulation, etc., depends upon the answer given
> to this question—how are men going to get together on this
> shrinking planet? The salvation men seek today is precisely
> the ability to get together in a way that will last. . . . Every-
> thing depends on man's determination to seek out and meet
> his brother in an effort to share with him.[9]

At a time in the Church when social activism was being promoted as the thing that every Catholic should be engaged in,
Clark and Martin were saying that the first and greatest priority for the universal Church and those who had experienced the
grace of conversion was to build authentic Christian communities. In a world in which Christian values were not supported
and were in fact often strongly opposed, they believed it was
more imperative than ever that spiritually renewed Christians
join together and support each other in daily life.

Clark and Martin proposed that the world could be changed
only by the witness of such people living united in Christ and
his Spirit. Covenant communities were a light shining in the

---

8. This was referred to in the annotated bibliography of Clark's book,
Building Christian Communities: Strategy for Renewing the Church (Notre
Dame, IN: Ave Maria Press, 1972), 188. Delespesse's book was entitled *The
Church Community: Leaven and Life-Style* (Ottawa, Canada: The Catholic
Centre of St. Paul University, 1969).

9. Delespesse, *The Church Community*, xi.

darkness (see Philippians 2:15), a sign of Christians' love for one another (see John 13:35). These communities could also be powerful instruments for service and evangelization, but Clark's emphasis was on their own intrinsic value: they reveal the true nature of the Church itself as community.

Delespesse defined community this way: "A community is an organic and stable fraternal association of persons accepting responsibility for one another, through sharing both what they are and what they have, in order to bring about the union of mankind."[10] A *Christian* community would then be a network of committed relationships among Christians to bring about the unity of mankind in the kingdom of God. Covenant agreements differed among communities, but the key was mutual love and service. As a document from the Word of God community explained,

> Coming into community means passing from relationships based primarily on my convenience or my need, to relationships that are based on commitment: Whether it's convenient or not, whether I need you or not, I commit myself to be a brother or sister to you. . . . We pass from a position of independence into a shared life. Living together under one roof or putting our salaries and material possessions in common are not essential aspects of community life. The relationship of brotherhood and

10. Ibid., 4.

sisterhood with each other is essential. It can be expressed in a variety of ways.[11]

One of the ways in which the Word of God functioned as a "family" was by providing services for its members and for those outside the community. These included weekday child-care and youth activity programs, facilities and services for guests, retreats, teaching courses, conferences, and provision for guidance and personal direction.

This experiment in covenant community in the Renewal caught the attention of Cardinal Suenens, who paid a visit to the Word of God in Ann Arbor, traveling incognito as a simple priest. He later visited the covenant community at Notre Dame. (I remember when our men's household was asked to perform a little skit for the cardinal about our community. It was a humbling experience.) The cardinal's experience and views are reflected in his book *A New Pentecost?*. First published in French in 1974, the cardinal introduced the chapter on the Holy Spirit and new communities with this quote from Steve Clark: "What the Church needs today, more than new institution or programs, are vital Christian communities."[12]

In this chapter, Cardinal Suenens observed that besides the fact that Christianity is "essentially communal," today a believer

11. Information obtained from "The Word of God," a mimeographed information sheet distributed by the Word of God community, Ann Arbor, Michigan, n.d. Obtained by the author in the fall of 1977.

12. Cardinal Leon-Joseph Suenens, *A New Pentecost?*, trans. Francis Martin (New York: Seabury Press, 1974), 136.

must "find again community life not only to live his faith but to survive as a Christian in a world growing more and more estranged from Christianity." Acknowledging that there is confusion about what "Christian community" means, Cardinal Suenens wrote that Jesus Christ is the cornerstone and foundation of every Christian community, and that all authentic renewal in the Church is "first and foremost a fresh discovery, of all that is implied in an intimate and personal relationship between Jesus Christ and the believer."[13] Suenens saw, in agreement with Martin, Clark, and other Renewal leaders, that the renewal of the Church—and even its very future—depended upon revitalized Christian communities, which must be built by spiritually renewed Christians who know Jesus intimately and personally:

> To a large degree, the renewal of the Church will begin when Christian communities become places of light and warmth for those around them. From a human point of view, it might seem paradoxical to make the future of the Church dependent upon small Christian communities which, no matter how fervent, are but a drop in the ocean. This is true. But if we consider the spiritual energy released by every group which allows Christ to fill it with the life of his Holy Spirit, then the perspective changes, for we are putting ourselves in the strength and power of God. The "little flock" of the Gospel is the symbol of the Christian minority, that minority which

---

13. Ibid., 145.

Dom Hélder Câmara likes to call the "Abraham" minority.
It is minorities, in fact, which change the world.[14]

This conviction underlies the passionate commitment that
many early leaders of the Renewal had to building Christian
covenant communities and why so many of these communities sprang up within the first decade of the Renewal. Steve
Clark's initial book on the importance of building Christian
community was followed by others. In one, he studies the
early monastic communities to see how they produced some
prominent lay leaders, many of whom were later ordained and
eventually became bishops. In another, Clark presents a modern-day rule for covenant community life, based on a dozen
years of experience and experimentation.[15]

My Own Experience of Covenant Community

What has been the fruit of the covenant communities in the
Renewal? Have they been "places of light and warmth for
those around them?" My own experience of being a member of two such communities for over forty years of my adult
life causes me to be very grateful to the Lord and to all the
brothers and sisters in Christ with whom I (with my wife and

14. Ibid., 153.

15. Stephen B. Clark, *Unordained Elders and Renewal Communities*
(New York: Paulist Press, 1976) and *Patterns of Christian Community:
A Statement of Community Order*, ed. Stephen B. Clark (Ann Arbor, MI:
Servant Publications, 1984), respectively.

children) have shared this life. As a young adult, I benefited from the practical wisdom that I received, both from programmatic community teaching and from the teaching and pastoral advice of leaders, who were laypeople, religious, and priests. One example was a twelve-week course called "Foundations of Christian Living," a formation course in the community I was part of during my college years at Notre Dame. Even though I had received good Catholic formation at home and in Catholic schools, the teaching of this course on, among other things, ordering one's life according to gospel values, Christian relationships, and speech was tremendously valuable to me, so much so that after I went through the course, I volunteered to tape it the next time it was presented just so I could hear it again. (And, I might add, I graduated with a theology degree from Notre Dame and found nothing fundamentalist or contrary to Catholic teaching in those courses; in fact, they supplemented and reinforced much of what I learned in the college classroom.)

As I matured and began my career and marriage, covenant community provided support for me from other Catholics who, like me, desired to live our Catholic faith vibrantly, both in the world and at home. I hope I was able to support them as well. And yet life in covenant community is sometimes challenging. It is not an attempt to create a utopian society, because we are all sinners, and the closer the contact you have with other people, the more clearly you can see their weaknesses, sins, and faults, as well as your own. But you also experience their goodness. Being in a good, healthy community is like having a healthy and supportive extended family. For those in this type of Christian community, the Church can never be seen as just a place where one goes on Sunday and other special occasions to obtain grace; it is a network of committed relationships in which Christ is present in our midst, as he promised (see Matthew 18:20).

There are other ways that covenant communities have contributed, and continue to contribute, to the Church. In the years immediately following the Second Vatican Council, the Catholic Church began a concerted effort to work more strenuously for the restoration of unity among Christians. In the Renewal, we have noted how Catholics learned much from their contact with other Christians, especially Pentecostals and neo-Pentecostal Protestant Christians. As one who attended the 1977 Conference on the Charismatic Renewal in the Christian Churches in Kansas City, Missouri, I will never forget this gathering of charismatic Christians, composed of Catholics, Lutherans, Mennonites, Presbyterians, United Methodists, Episcopalians, Messianic Jews, classical Pentecostals, and nondenominational charismatic Christians. While each group had its own sessions during the day, all participants met together each evening in Arrowhead Stadium to worship and hear God's word proclaimed. The planning committee was chaired by Dr. Kevin Ranaghan and administered by Charismatic Renewal Services, based in South Bend. Again, the leadership and resources of covenant communities in the Renewal made this event possible.

In addition, some prayer groups and covenant communities in the Renewal are ecumenical; that is, their membership includes Christians from different traditions who acknowledge their differences in belief and practice but realize that, as Pope St. John XXIII said, what we share in common is much greater than what divides us. Over the years, Catholic involvement in grassroots ecumenical efforts (including ecumenical prayer groups) has waned, and yet covenant communities that started out ecumenical by and large still remain so today, as a witness that Christians from different traditions can share a committed common life.

In Catholic circles today, Sherry Weddell has popularized the concept of "intentional discipleship"—people making a conscious decision to follow Christ and allowing that decision to guide every aspect of their lives. Entering into a covenant commitment in a charismatic community is a form of intentional discipleship that we have seen in the Renewal for almost fifty years.[16]

Covenant Communities: Challenges and Trials

Founding, maintaining, and living in a covenant community is not easy. It is like a religious community in those aspects because it requires commitment, a leadership structure, and a

---

16. It should be noted that this covenant is entered into freely and voluntarily. Covenant communities in the Renewal are not cults that coerce members into joining. They attract members by their way of life. It is a sociological truth that peer pressure can keep a person in a community, and some covenant communities have advised people not to leave a community because they believed that God's action and power are there in a special way. But covenant community membership is intentional and voluntary.

defined way of life, all of which ensure stability and continuity over time. Anyone who has studied in detail the history of religious communities in the Catholic Church knows that they all go through trials and struggles, both internal and external. Covenant communities are no different, and in some ways there are more challenges because there are not as many models of highly committed groups that are predominantly lay in membership. Most religious communities are composed of people committed to celibacy. There are "third order" groups, which are predominantly lay but are usually not as all-encompassing in the extent and degree of commitment of the members to each other and their way of life as many covenant communities are, or at least as they were in their origins.

What are the challenges faced by covenant communities in the Renewal? One of the most common criticisms of these covenant communities has been that they are rigid and elitist—too structured and too concerned about their own community life and affairs. Perhaps the greatest temptation or spiritual pitfall of covenant communities and their members, especially in the first ten to twenty years of the Renewal, was hubris (pride) and, closely related to it, elitism. Pride is often a subtle temptation, and in the Renewal it usually arose from a joyful and grateful sense of discovering a fuller Christian life. The temptation that corrupted that good sentiment was to become inordinately absorbed in one's life in community, and even (perhaps only subconsciously) to begin to look down on other Catholics, such as the average Catholic parishioner, as having a deficient or subpar Christian life. That's pride. (Please remember that I'm speaking of a temptation; not all members of covenant communities thought this way.)

There were prophecies that came in the late 1970s about covenant communities being a bulwark for the Church—a source of strength and protection. (This is not to be confused with a remnant—that would imply that only they were faithful to God and would be the "elect," the "chosen," or the "saved.") Again, being a bulwark against evil is a good thing, but it *could* lead to a sense of false pride or elitism.

Regarding elitism, since covenant community members had very full lives because of the commitment to prayer, service, and group meetings, it was easy for those outside these communities to think of covenant community members as elitists who were busy (perhaps *too* busy) about their own affairs. (Being judgmental can go both ways.) Now, if we were talking about a Catholic *religious* community, most people would understand that consecrated religious have chosen a way of life that cuts them off, to a certain extent, from the world, because their lives are more focused on God and the apostolate or mission of their religious community. But because covenant communities are made up mostly of laypeople, we think it unusual for them to be so focused on religious commitments or service within the community itself and also its apostolates. So the judgment of those outside that covenant communities were elitist or some sort of strange sect may have been based on certain preconceived notions of how laypeople ought to be spending their time and what their interests should be. On the other hand, *if* covenant community members were actually so focused on their community life that they had no time for or interest in spending time with or serving those outside their community, the charge of elitism might fit.

It has also been noted that some of the models of covenant community (such as Steve Clark's) were based on monastic life or other forms of religious life designed for celibates. In some covenant communities, there were groups or households designed for those considering or committed to celibate life that were highly structured and dedicated to service. Sometimes these were called or considered "brotherhood" or "sisterhood" groups or households.

This model of community life has its place, but it isn't immediately transferable to covenant community life for married couples and families. When demands on these groups became too heavy (and each couple or family has a different capacity for commitments and service outside the home), sometimes this caused difficulties. This pastoral issue undoubtedly was approached in different ways in different communities, but it was at least a danger that married couples, especially those with children, in covenant communities would experience undue stress on account of the demands of life in an active, committed community. Some would feel guilty if they could not meet their perceived obligations or were going through a period of struggle of some sort. Covenant communities did raise the bar of expectation of what a full Christian life could or ought to look like, but sometimes that bar was too high for particular individuals or families, at least for a period of time.

I would add that some communities learned from this experience to be more flexible and to encourage their members to exercise their own good judgment about how much they were able to do regarding community life and commitments.

Pastoral Care and Leadership in Covenant Communities

One provision for helping members of covenant community to live a vibrant and yet healthy and balanced life in covenant community is a system of pastoral care. "Pastor/shepherd" was one of the charisms listed in the New Testament letters, and in the Renewal, there is a belief that even laypeople are given pastoral gifts by God that should be used for the good of others. In the early years, many covenant communities had pastoral leaders (sometimes called "heads") who gave pastoral advice on matters in the lives of the members of their group. In the Catholic tradition, a spiritual director sometimes has this role, even in the lives of laypeople, but the availability of trained spiritual directors in the Church today is limited. So some covenant communities developed a pastoral care system to help people discern God's will and direction for their lives and to share wisdom and insight that could help a person grow both spiritually and in their relationships with others.

However, problems arose in some communities, related especially to the intensity of community life and the area of pastoral care. Members of some communities experienced their covenant community life as becoming burdensome. Others experienced pastoral care as personally intrusive or believed poor or mistaken advice was being given, and sometimes it was being presented as authoritative and God's will, not just advice. Some people giving pastoral care or advice had little or no training or formation for this role even though the overall community leaders discerned that they had pastoral abilities or charisms. It was a challenge to provide good formation and instruction for pastoral leaders, and sometimes too much was expected of them. There were failures.

As a result, some members left covenant communities, often embittered by their bad experience. It must be said in fairness that some people who were attracted to and joined these communities wanted and needed more or different help dealing with issues in their own lives or families than the pastoral care in community could realistically provide, and sometimes this was not recognized. Pastoral leaders usually were compassionate and did their best to help brothers and sisters in Christ work through their situations with prayer, encouragement, and advice. (Isn't this what *ought* to be happening in the body of Christ?) Eventually, some community members raised concerns such as these about communities and brought them to the attention of their bishops or pastors. At times, this resulted in investigations to determine whether there were abuses occurring in these communities.

A number of covenant communities in the United States have undergone a period of internal struggles that led either to the renewal and reform of the community, divisions into different communities, or even the demise of the community. The True House community at Notre Dame was disbanded in the mid-1970s as a result of the intervention of the leaders of other covenant communities because of a serious leadership issue. This action of self-regulation by covenant communities in such a young movement is, to me, a sign of the Renewal's strength and maturity.

In the early 1990s, a number of covenant communities in the United States underwent difficult times. In my own experience, some members of the Servants of Christ the King community in Steubenville went to the local bishop to express their concerns, especially regarding pastoral care. After a review of the community initiated by the bishop, he directed the community to make certain changes. The community willingly followed all of the bishop's directives, and its life continued, though some members formed another small community, while others left the community, and some even left the Renewal itself. It was a painful and difficult time, but it was a pruning process that enabled the community, following the bishop's directives, to resolve the pastoral problems that were at issue. In the end, after the investigation the original community came together again and took the name "Community of God's Love," which had been the original name of the prayer group and early covenant community. "We know that in everything God works for good with those who love him" (Romans 8:28).

Similar ecclesial reviews were undertaken in other covenant communities, such as the Mother of God community in Maryland, but no other community I know of was ordered to disband, and all submitted to the directives of the bishop.

Looking back, there are many things that these covenant communities and the Renewal as a whole have learned, especially from these periods of hardship. We know that not even the power of God or the abundant outpouring of the Holy Spirit, as seen in the charisms, exempts any group in the Church from temptation, struggle, and even seeming failure. St. Paul rebukes the most "charismatic" local Christian church that he addresses, the church in Corinth, for the serious divisions among them (1 Corinthians 3:5) and corrects them for not valuing *all* the charisms of the members of their church (12:14-26). Of course, Paul also teaches that "suffering produces endurance, and endurance produces character, and character produces hope, and hope does not disappoint us, because God's love has been poured into our hearts through the Holy Spirit who has been given to us" (Romans 5:3-5).

What individual, parish, church community, or religious order has not experienced suffering or trials, sometimes as a result of their own sins and weakness? I look upon the trials of the covenant communities and the Renewal as a whole as a way of God pruning the Renewal so that we would bear more and better fruit for God's kingdom. Sometimes these trials may also be a type of spiritual warfare, because Satan is certainly not pleased when Christians commit their lives more deeply to each other and open themselves more to the gifts and the power of God, as we see in these communities. Whatever the cause of these trials, they can produce endurance, character, and hope when they are accepted and endured in faith.

Finally, in mentioning the pain caused by divisions, we recognize that divisions and difficulties have arisen among leaders in the Renewal that have led to some parting of ways between covenant communities. For example, in the United States, at the beginning of the formation of covenant communities, there was an emerging "association" of communities. In 1978 a difference in vision among some leaders led to some covenant communities forming an international alliance called the "Sword of the Spirit," while the People of Praise in South Bend developed associated branch communities following their model of community life. In 1990 the Word of God in Ann Arbor withdrew from the Sword of the Spirit alliance. Some members of the Word of God chose to remain allied with the Sword of the Spirit and adopted the name "the Word of Life." As of June 2016, the Sword of the Spirit had seventy-five communities in twenty-six countries with a total of nine thousand people in these communities.

Another major grouping of covenant communities in the Renewal emerged when some communities desired to emphasize their Catholic identity and forge a closer, formal alliance with the Catholic Church. One of the first of the covenant communities in the United States that moved in this direction was the Community of God's Delight in Dallas. Other communities from around the world joined this alliance, including the Emmanuel Community in Brisbane, Australia. Established in 1990, this alliance was named the Catholic Fraternity of Charismatic Covenant Communities and Fellowships and was decreed an international association of the faithful of Pontifical

Right. As of June 2016, the Catholic Fraternity comprises fifty-one communities in fourteen countries—two in Asia, six in Europe, three in South America, and the rest in Australia, Canada, and the U.S.

These different alliances of covenant communities could be seen as unfortunate divisions, and it is unfortunate and sad if they see themselves as opposed to each other or somehow in competition. However, the current situation could be seen as the Lord producing more richness in the diversity of calls and missions of these communities and their alliances and groupings. Even when the emergence of these different alliances sometimes came as a result of differences and disagreements among the leaders of these communities and sometimes their members as well, if later there was reconciliation among them, we can recognize the Lord bringing good even out of what seemed at the time to be unfortunate and regrettable division. This has happened many times in the history of religious life, as new communities and orders have been founded by leaders who felt a new calling or a somewhat different calling within a tradition.

Prayer Groups in the Renewal

As we have seen, from the first years of the Renewal, the leadership in the first hubs of the Renewal—South Bend/Notre Dame and Ann Arbor—focused their pastoral efforts on promoting the Renewal and building covenant communities, whose resources made possible the publications and conferences that gave the Renewal direction and the resources of talented and committed people. However, a study published in 1983, at a time covenant communities when were at their peak, noted,

> Approximately 96 percent of the renewal consists of prayer groups—most of which have some kind of parish contact— and the vast majority of these people would never seriously consider abandoning their present life styles for the total environment of the Christian community.[17]

The researchers of the 1983 study, Richard J. Bord and Joseph E. Faulkner, noted that each prayer group had its own leaders with a wide range of leadership styles because they had a great deal of autonomy to organize and determine events. They found three kinds of leadership in prayer groups: strong lay leadership, strong clerical leadership, and relatively weak lay leadership. According to this study, the first type is more autonomous in relationship to Church authority and may be attracted to a deeper, covenant relationship. The second type is more closely linked to the Church and may have more emphasis on being Catholic than charismatic. Those in leadership were generally those "willing to devote the required time and effort," with the emphasis "on service as a criterion of leadership."[18]

---

17. Richard J. Bord and Joseph E. Faulkner, *The Catholic Charismatics: The Anatomy of a Modern Religious Movement* (University Park, PA: Pennsylvania State University Press, 1983), 139.

18. Ibid., 17–18.

One of the chronic challenges for prayer groups is lack of stability. This is sometimes referred to as the "revolving door" syndrome where people, even leaders, come and go because no long-term commitment is required.

My own involvement in prayer groups began in 1970, when I returned to my hometown for the summer only a couple of months after I was baptized in the Spirit. I realized my need for support and growth, and I asked the Lord to provide this. After attending a weekday Mass in my parish, I noticed a few people staying in the pews together after Mass, praying. Somehow I sensed I should speak with them when they finished praying. It turned out they were charismatics who had started a weekly prayer meeting in one of their homes a couple of blocks from the parish. They invited me to attend. I went almost every week all summer, and it was a blessing—just what I needed to grow in Christ at the time. I continued to keep in contact with this group when I visited home, even after graduating from college, but was saddened that two of the strongest male leaders left the Catholic Church. Without much acceptance or support for their charismatic life in their parish, which was served by two priests who had no interest in supporting the group, they had decided to leave. Later when I went home, I attended a prayer group supported by and held in a retreat house run by the Cenacle sisters. The wisdom and charity of the sisters helped make this a rich experience of Catholic charismatic worship.

My other prayer-group exposure was during my three-and-a-half years as a graduate student in Toronto, Canada. A large prayer group met weekly in the undercroft of St. Basil's Church on the campus of the University of St. Michael's College in the heart of downtown Toronto, where I was studying. The group attracted a diverse cross section of people; perhaps two hundred met weekly. The core team that ran the meeting was made up of both women and men who worked and related together well. It was a refreshing time of charismatic prayer, teaching, and fellowship, and some of my closest friendships during that time developed with members of the prayer group. We were blessed to have some excellent teachers, such as Fr. George Montague, who was rector of the Marianist seminarians at St. Basil's Seminary right across the street. It was a good example of a prayer group that provided vibrant worship, good teaching, and supportive fellowship.

As in my experience, some prayer groups met in homes, while others met in churches, parish halls, or religious houses. The vision for many of these groups was to offer Life in the Spirit Seminars (or the equivalent) to introduce people to life in the Holy Spirit and pray with them to be baptized in the Spirit and then to provide a setting for charismatic prayer, spiritual support, and fellowship.

The Charismatic Renewal in Parishes

In addition to building community through covenant communities and prayer groups, others believed that the Renewal had the potential to renew Catholic parish life or at least thought that the Renewal should be integrated into parish life. Actually, there could be a big difference between those two visions. The first vision would be a "charismatically renewed" parish in which the power of the Holy Spirit (through baptism in the Holy Spirit) and the charisms would be seen as a normal, accepted part of parish life. The second vision would be that prayer meetings should be a normal, accepted activity in the parish, like the Holy Name Society or the Catholic women's club—available for those interested in charismatic prayer and using charisms in worship.

The question is often posed, "What is the goal or the purpose of this Renewal in God's plan?" The most common response is that the Renewal should be integrated into the life of the Church and thus eventually disappear as a distinct movement. We will discuss this more in the book's final chapter, but it raises an important question: what does it mean to be "integrated" into the life of the Church? Does it mean, as in the first vision, that parishes should be "charismatically renewed" so that it would be normal for Catholics in any typical parish to have their Christian initiation renewed through baptism in the Holy Spirit, and to have their various charisms recognized and used in the context of the parish liturgy and ordinary parish functions? Or does integration into the life of the Church mean that each parish should have a prayer group (or access to a prayer group) supported by the pastor, his associates and deacons, and the pastoral council of the parish, which all parishioners would be encouraged (or at least welcome) to attend?

While the first vision might seem unrealistic, there have been instances in which the pastor's plan, or at least his hope, was to have a charismatic renewal of the whole parish. In some cases, this, or something like it, actually has happened. One of the most intriguing and powerful accounts is the story of the renewal of St. Patrick's Parish Community in Providence, Rhode Island, in the late 1960s and early 1970s, which is recounted by Fr. John Randall in his book *In God's Providence: The Birth of a Catholic Charismatic Parish*. Fr. Randall noted that "if it ever were going to prove itself, [the Renewal] would have to show what it could do in transforming a parish, a territorial parish, an ordinary parish."[19] He proposed such a parish to his bishop, who to his surprise accepted the idea, and he was named pastor of St. Patrick's Parish Community. The Renewal was key to building this parish:

> The Lord wants us to concentrate on building up the St. Patrick's Parish Community that it might be a city on the mountain, a light that can't be hidden, a parish that's come alive through the Charismatic Renewal, giving hope to other parishes that it can be done, not by men, not even by the joint efforts of men, but by God Who gives the growth

---

19. John Randall, *In God's Providence: The Birth of a Catholic Charismatic Parish* (Plainfield, NJ: Logos, 1973), 41.

in all circumstances. Unless the Lord builds the city, they labor in vain who build it (cf. Psalm 127).[20]

Other accounts of a similar nature, though each unique in its details, were presented at a think tank on parish renewal held in the fall of 1987 at Franciscan University of Steubenville. The event was sponsored by the Fraternity of Priests, a charismatic organization for the mutual support of priests, and featured a number of testimonies of how the Renewal had been instrumental or central in the renewal of parishes.

Based on this meeting, Kevin Perrotta wrote an article recounting the stories of the renewal of St. Alphonsus Church in Langdon, North Dakota (Frs. Ken Gallagher and Tony Salzbrunn), St. Mary's Parish, Ottawa, Ontario, Canada (Fr. Bob Bedard, who was also the founder of a charismatic order of priests, the Companions of the Cross), and St. Boniface Church near Fort Lauderdale, Florida (Fr. Michael Eivers and Deacon Perry Vitale). The think tank proposed no formula or program for parish renewal though the Renewal. Not surprisingly, the key to the renewal of all these parishes was responding

---

20. Ibid., 71. On page 145 of *The Catholic Charismatics*, Bord and Faulkner include a sobering comment regarding these experiences in charismatic parish renewal: "Randall is well aware that his charismatically renewed parish is unique. He acknowledges that parish renewal is not likely unless the local pastor is the head of the parish prayer group, which is extremely rare. Pastors have a vested interest in the traditional forms of worship and have little to gain by promoting prayer groups in their parishes; in fact, they risk a great deal by siding with what is usually a poorly understood and a somewhat extreme minority in the parish. It is unlikely that parish renewal along CCR lines will make headlines in the near future."

faithfully to the Holy Spirit, although Perrotta mentioned that one "programmatic element" in all three parishes was the eventual establishment of small groups for mutual support of parishioners. Other common elements included the following:

> That very elementary activity of telling the gospel, inviting people to place their lives under the lordship of Christ and to expect the action of his Spirit, was the crucial activity that all these pastors devoted themselves to. And before calling others to do it, they had done it themselves.
>
> Also, as the Spirit acted, they followed. The patterns of evangelism and conversion were different in each church, but in every case the pastors cooperated with what they saw God doing. They were willing to go to great lengths to cooperate.[21]

In all these cases, the priests involved had to step out of the mold of what was expected in normal parish life, which took courage and faith. They had to act on faith to do what they believed God was calling them to do, which required a real openness to the Holy Spirit in their own personal and priestly lives. The fruit of this openness was the building of parish communities that learned with their priests what it meant to trust in the Lord and to be open to the Holy Spirit as a parish community. Isn't this how the communities in the early Church operated and grew? One of the challenges of this approach, of course, is that when a pastor who has a particular vision (such

---

21. Kevin Perrotta, "Catholic Parishes and the Holy Spirit," *Pastoral Renewal* 12, No. 7 (1988), 16.

as for a "charismatically renewed" parish) leaves the parish, the vision will inevitably die unless the pastors who succeed him understand, embrace, and actively promote this vision. In practice, this seldom occurs unless the very "culture" of the parish is changed to embrace the charismatic dimension, and succeeding pastors continue to support and foster it.

Some leaders in the Renewal in the 1970s sought to chart a course that centered around parish renewal. George Martin (no relation to Ralph), in his book *Parish Renewal: A Charismatic Approach,* begins by stating:

> The goal of the charismatic renewal within the Catholic Church is a charismatically renewed Catholic Church. The ultimate aim is not to have a successful and thriving Catholic charismatic movement, but to have a complete renewal of Christian life in the power of the Spirit. The charismatic renewal is in the Church and for the Church. Its purpose is the renewal of the Church.
>
> If these are basic principles to guide the charismatic renewal today, we must apply them to parish life. To relate properly to the Church as a whole, the charismatic renewal must establish a correct relationship to the local parish, and bring renewal to the parish. The charismatic renewal will not have its full impact on the Church unless it plays a role in parish renewal.[22]

---

22. George Martin, *Parish Renewal: A Charismatic Approach* (Ann Arbor, MI: Word of Life, 1976), 1.

Martin's approach, according to researchers Bord and Faulkner, is the model of a "cheerful servant"—participants active in the Renewal who "immerse themselves vigorously and cheerfully in worthwhile parish activities." These individuals "serve as models to those outside the [Renewal]," with the hope that "they can stimulate a general parish renewal."[23]

Another Renewal leader who believed that the Renewal needed a more parish-based emphasis, and who also was critical of elitist tendencies he saw in the Renewal, was Fr. Joseph Lange, OSFS. With Anthony Cushing, he published a four-volume set of books called *Living Christian Community*. Noting that one of the common observation of Renewal participants is that their parish seems "dead," he writes,

> Look at the people in your "dead" church. Do you really know where they are with God? Do you have any right to judge? . . .
>
> Once we recognize how weak and miserable we are, even with the Holy Spirit, then we can see that others, too, can have the Spirit but in a different way. I do not mean that all of us are not meant to have the baptism of the Spirit. But I do mean that the absence of this, that, or the other manifestation of the Spirit does not mean that the Spirit is absent altogether.
>
> We are Christians because we believe and are baptized into the Body of Christ. We are all maturing in Christ. We are all growing differently. Let us see the Spirit in each other. What a different experience we would have in our churches if only we

---

23. Bord and Faulkner, *The Catholic Charismatics*, 144–145.

would look for the good in each other and rejoice in it, instead of judging one another and putting each other down.[24]

Although Lange is correct about the need not to judge others, many charismatics insist that God is pouring out his Spirit so that Catholics will have fuller life in the Spirit. They ask, "How long will Catholics have to settle for spiritually insipid parish life?"

In another book, Lange presents his own constructive vision for parish renewal.

> I have seen Cursillistas, Marriage Encounter people, and Charismatics become the backbone of parishes, becoming leaven, working quietly, praying and giving. A constantly recurring problem, though, is the attempt to manipulate the pastor into changing. The Christian process is altogether different. It is the way of love. Look for the good and affirm it. Rejoice in it. Make a friend and be a friend to your pastor. Don't expect to be believed until you have become believable. Offer your priest the understanding and the desire to understand without judging. Above all, think in terms of years, not in terms of weeks.[25]

24. Joseph Lange, OSFS, and Anthony Cushing, *Worshipping Community, Living Christian Community Series, Vol. 2* (Pecos, NM: Dove Publications, 1975), 41–42.

25. Joseph Lange, OSFS, *Renewing the Catholic Parish* (Denville, NJ: Dimension Books, 1979), 82.

Again, while Lange is right in counseling patience, what about people who have been serving faithfully in parishes for many years and yet have seen little movement forward—little openness to the charisms or baptism in the Spirit in parish life? How long, O Lord?

Lange became editor of a magazine, *Catholic Charismatic,* which claimed to be more expressive of Catholic tradition than other periodicals that were available. Whether or not that was the case, the fact that, by the mid-1970s, there was room for two national magazines in the U.S. on the Catholic Charismatic Renewal reflects the growth and vitality of the Renewal in that time.

How was the Renewal to contribute to the overall renewal of life in Catholic parishes? In many places, people in the Renewal are satisfied (if not pleased) if they can attain the second "vision": to have permission and support for a charismatic prayer meeting or prayer group in their parish. Perhaps they even have a Mass in the parish occasionally in which people can receive prayer for healing, either during or after Mass, along with the Sacrament of the Anointing of the Sick for those who are eligible.

These things are a far cry from being a "charismatically renewed" parish, but they do provide for some form of charismatic community or fellowship within the parish. It should be noted that, at least in the United States, the number of parish-based prayer groups has steadily declined in recent years. The first "vision"—a parish in which opportunities for baptism in the Holy Spirit and exercise of the charisms both in the liturgy and in normal parish life abound—can be achieved only through the leadership of the pastor and/or priests of the parish with the permission of the local bishop. We have considered past examples of this, and more recent cases will be presented in our final chapter. The real difficulty is that parish pastors and priests do not remain in one parish forever, and bishops change as well. As a result, the status of the Renewal in a particular parish is always, at present, temporary and contingent.

Put simply, without the support of the bishops and priests, no renewal of the Church on the diocesan or parish level will take place. How has the Catholic hierarchy responded to the Renewal? That is the topic of our next chapter.

Chapter 6

The Catholic Hierarchy and the Renewal

Every movement or group in the Catholic Church is subject to the authority and guidance of the Church's pastors, especially the pope and the bishops, who make up the Church's primary hierarchy or leadership structure. In regard to these movements, the heirarchy's role is to "test everything" (1 Thessalonians 5:21) or to "test the spirits to see whether they are of God" (1 John 4:1), as well as to provide pastoral guidance and support for individual Catholics involved in these movements or groups.

So what has the Catholic hierarchy had to say about the Catholic Charismatic Renewal? We have already seen that the Second Vatican Council (1962–1965) taught about the importance and the role of charisms in the Church. Vatican II's *Presbyterorum Ordinis* [Decree on the Ministry and Life of Priests] speaks directly about how ordained ministers should pastor the charisms and the lay members of the Church who possess them: "While trying the spirits to see if they be of God, they must discover with faith, recognize with joy, and foster with diligence the many and varied charismatic gifts of the laity, whether these be of a humble or more exalted kind" (9).

This document, promulgated on December 7, 1965, shows how God was preparing the hierarchy of the Church to discern and support the Renewal that emerged a little over a year later.

A New Pentecost

Pope St. John XXIII was the prophetic pope who called the Second Vatican Council, and on December 25, 1961, exhorted the whole Church to pray for the upcoming council with a prayer that began, "Renew Your wonders in our time, as though for a new Pentecost." Shortly before his death, he predicted that after the council "will dawn that new Pentecost which is the object of our yearning."[1]

Blessed Pope Paul VI brought the council to a conclusion after Pope St. John XXIII's death in 1963 and presided over the Catholic Church during the emergence of the Renewal until his death in 1978. Paul VI aligned himself with Pope St. John XXIII in his hope for a new Pentecost. Toward the end of his pontificate, in 1975, he wrote,

> One must . . . recognize a prophetic intuition on the part of
> our predecessor, John XXIII, who envisioned a kind of new
> Pentecost as a fruit of the Council. We too have wished to
> place ourself in the same perspective and in the same attitude

1. John XXIII, Address on the Closing of the First Conciliar Session, December 8, 1962, https://w2.vatican.va/content/john-xxiii/la/speeches/1962/documents/hf_j-xxiii_spe_19621208_closing-i-period.html; my translation.

of expectation. Not that Pentecost has ever ceased to be an actuality throughout the entire history of the Church, but so great are the needs and perils of the present age, so vast the horizons of mankind drawn towards world coexistence and powerless to achieve it, that there is no salvation for it except in a new outpouring of the gift of God. Let Him then come, the Creating Spirit, to renew the face of the earth![2]

Even before the Renewal emerged, Pope Paul VI had a pastoral concern to increase Catholics' awareness of the person of the Holy Spirit. In 1964, he revised the Divine Praises recited during Benediction, adding the phrase, "Blessed be the Holy Spirit, the Paraclete."[3] On October 12, 1966, he declared, "If we really love the Church, the main thing we must do is to foster an outpouring of the Divine Paraclete." In that same speech, he said that "the Church's first need is always to live Pentecost."[4]

Fr. Edward O'Connor, CSC, author of *Pope Paul and the Spirit*, summarizes Pope Paul VI's views on devotion to the Holy Spirit:

Pope Paul may well have done more to promote devotion to the Holy Spirit than perhaps any other Pope in history. While he has not composed any single document surveying the whole

2. Paul VI, *Gaudete in Domino* [On Christian Joy], May 9, 1975, https://w2.vatican.va/content/paul-vi/en/apost_exhortations/documents/hf_p-vi_exh_19750509_gaudete-in-domino.html.

3. Edward D. O'Connor, CSC, *Pope Paul and the Spirit* (Notre Dame, IN: Ave Maria Press, 1978), 3.

4. Ibid., 6, 7.

theology of the Spirit, as Leo XIII did, he has spoken insistently and eloquently on this subject throughout the whole course of his pontificate. Joyously he proclaims the fact that the Spirit has been poured out on us by the Risen Christ; in rich detail and from various points of view he describes the workings and gifts of the Spirit; he constantly exhorts his hearers to seek and prepare for them. Again and again he recommends devotion to the Holy Spirit as the greatest of all devotions (April 26, 1964), the first devotion (May 18, 1967) and the summit of devotion (May 26, 1971). "The work of the Holy Spirit," he says, "is decisive for the Christian religion" (May 17, 1972).[5]

Pope Paul VI and the Renewal

Paul VI not only promoted devotion to the Holy Spirit, but when the Charismatic Renewal emerged in the Catholic Church, he did many things to encourage and guide it. O'Connor points out that "Paul is the first Pope to use the term *charismatic* as a usual part of his vocabulary." He continues,

> He also speaks much more freely than his predecessors of the "prophetic" aspect of the Church. Up to Vatican II, Catholic doctrine had reserved this term almost exclusively for the official teaching office in the Church; but Pope Paul likes to use it in a broader and livelier sense, as when he seeks to arouse in his hearers "the prophetic spark of witnessing,"

---

5. Ibid., 7.

and reminds them that on Pentecost, "the Apostles are filled with prophetic breath to proclaim the amazing, innovative event: Christ has risen from the dead."[6]

O'Connor notes that Paul VI frequently summoned Christians "to a living, personal faith in Jesus, and calls on them to be joyous and enthusiastic in their faith." In addition,

> He insists that scripture is a living word, by which God speaks to us here and now. He urges us to take our questions to the God present within us (June 23, 1971), because the Holy Spirit speaks to those who know how to listen to him (May 25, 1969). He stresses the importance of bearing witness to Christ, but adds that, in order to be able to do this effectively, we must first have the inner witness of the Holy Spirit in our own hearts (May 24, 1972).[7]

This theme of the importance of the Holy Spirit for evangelization was developed by Paul VI in his apostolic exhortation *Evangelii Nuntiandi* [On Evangelization in the Modern World], promulgated on December 8, 1975. He called the Holy Spirit "the principal agent of evangelization" and said that "evangelization will never be possible" without him. Even the best techniques "resting on a sociological or psychological basis are quickly seen to be quite valueless" without the Holy Spirit's action (*Evangelii Nuntiandi*, 75).

---

6. Ibid., 12.

7. Ibid.

One would think that such a pope would immediately approve of the Renewal. However, Pope Paul was cautious because of previous movements in Christian history, such as Montanism, which viewed the institutional church as being at odds with, or even inferior to, the charismatic church. However, as Paul VI met with and came to know leaders of the Renewal, he warmed up to the movement as he saw that their spiritual fervor was pervaded by a deep love and loyalty to the Catholic Church. On February 21, 1973, he met with Cardinal Leon-Joseph Suenens, who first explained to him the nature of the Renewal in some detail.

On October 10, 1973, Pope Paul VI met with about 120 leaders of the Renewal from thirty-four countries who had assembled in Grottaferrata, Italy, just outside Rome. Two months later, addressing a gathering of cardinals, he remarked that

> the breath-giving influence of the Spirit has come to awaken latent forces within the Church, to stir up forgotten charisms, and to infuse that sense of vitality and joy which in every epoch of history marks the Church itself as youthful and up-to-date, ready and happy again to proclaim its eternal message to the modern age (December 21, 1973).[8]

In July 1974, Pope Paul VI spoke openly in a radio address about an "effusion" or "rain" of charisms that was appearing in the Church and noted that a new book by Cardinal Suenens (*A New Pentecost?*) "describes . . . the great expectation

---

8. Ibid., 41.

for a greater outpouring of supernatural graces, which are called charisms."[9] In doing so, Pope Paul was echoing what the Second Vatican Council had taught about the charisms and the Church's need to welcome them and be open to them.

The most public and telling indication of Pope Paul VI's views on the Renewal was certainly Pentecost Sunday 1975, when he celebrated Mass at St. Peter's Basilica with ten thousand people attending the International Conference on the Catholic Charismatic Renewal. Speaking as someone who was privileged to be present at that Mass, it was an event that I will never forget.

The significance of this event for the recognition of the Charismatic Renewal as a legitimate movement within the Catholic Church can't be overstated. The first official pastoral statement regarding the Renewal by any conference of Catholic bishops had been the U.S. Catholic bishops' statement in 1969. It was cautiously affirmative, taking a "wait and see" approach. Pope Paul's invitation for the Renewal to meet in Rome and to celebrate Mass with him at St. Peter's coincided with and encouraged a number of bishops' conferences around

---

9. Paul VI, quoted in *Open the Windows: The Popes and the Charismatic Renewal*, ed. Kilian McDonnell, OSB (South Bend, IN: Greenlawn Press, 1989), 8.

the world issuing basically affirmative statements about the Renewal in 1975 and the years shortly following.[10]

What did Pope Paul say to the Renewal at this momentous event? In his formal prepared text, a couple of lines stand out:

> Nothing is more necessary to this more and more secularized world than the witness of this "spiritual renewal" that we see the Holy Spirit evoking in the most diverse regions and milieus. . . . How then could this "spiritual renewal" not be "a chance" for the church and for the world? And how, in this case, could one not take all the means to ensure that it remains so?[11]

Pope Paul constantly bemoaned the decline of prayer and "interiority" and saw this fresh and powerful outpouring of the Holy Spirit as God's response to this—if we would accept it and be open to it. In this talk he also addressed the importance of the charisms and summarized St. Paul's teaching on them in three points, stressing the primacy of love above all (cf. 1 Corinthians 13).

When the Holy Father addressed the assembly in his native Italian, he reflected exuberantly on the name by which he knew

---

10. See *Presence, Power, Praise: Documents on the Charismatic Renewal, Vol. II*, ed. Kilian McDonnell, OSB (Collegeville, MN: Liturgical Press, 1980). Fr. McDonnell includes statements from Catholic bishops' conferences from the U.S. (1975), Australia (1975), Canada (1975), Belgium (1975), Costa Rica (1979), Germany (1979), and some regarding all of Latin America, promulgated at Puebla (1979).

11. McDonnell, *Open the Windows*, 12, 13.

us: "Spiritual Renewal" (or "Renewal in the Spirit," which the Renewal is still called in Italy).

> Reflect on the two-part name by which you are designated, "Spiritual Renewal." Where the Spirit is concerned, we are immediately alert, immediately happy to welcome the coming of the Holy Spirit. More than that, we invite him, we pray to him, we desire nothing more than that Christians, believing people, should experience an awareness, a worship, a greater joy through the Spirit of God among us. Have we forgotten the Holy Spirit? Certainly not! We want him, we honor him, we love him, and we invoke him. You, with your devotion and fervor, you wish to live in the Spirit. [applause] This [applause] . . . and this should be where the second part of your name comes in—a renewal. It ought to rejuvenate the world, give it back a spirituality, a soul, religious thought. It ought to reopen its closed lips to prayer and open its mouth to song, to joy, to hymns and to witnessing. It will be very fortuitous for our times, for our brothers, that there should be a generation, your generation of young people, who shout out to the world the glory and the greatness of the God of Pentecost.[12]

For a pope who was besieged with controversy over *Humanae Vitae* and many manifestations of dissent and unrest in the Church, this spiritual renewal—people who loved God and were loyal to the pope and the Catholic Church—was a breath

---

12. Ibid., 18.

of fresh air. Above all, Pope Paul VI consistently believed and taught, even before the Charismatic Renewal movement in the Catholic Church and his awareness of what it was all about, that renewed devotion to the Holy Spirit was important for the whole Church in our time. Perhaps Paul VI was surprised by the abundant outpouring of the Spirit and the reemergence of charisms in this movement, but he (like his predecessor, Pope St. John XXIII) had been praying for "a new Pentecost"—even though neither of them knew exactly what form it would take and from where it would come.[13]

Pope St. John Paul II and the Renewal

By 1978 the Renewal was in its heyday in the United States and was spreading throughout the world. In previous chapters, we have discussed covenant communities, the move of the ICCRS office from Belgium to Rome with Fr. Tom Forrest, CSSR, as director, and the founding of the Catholic Fraternity of Charismatic Covenant Communities and Fellowships. There were many other national and international ministries sparked by the Renewal in the late 1970s and early 1980s, such as the media outreach of the Community of God's Delight in Dallas, Mother Angelica's Eternal Word Television Network (EWTN) in Birmingham, Alabama, which initially had firm and fruitful roots in the Renewal, the International Catholic Program

---

13. There were, of course, many other manifestations of the "new Pentecost" in the Church, such as other spiritual renewal movements that were not explicitly charismatic.

of Evangelization (ICPE) in Malta, founded by Mario and Henry Cappello, and Ralph Martin's Renewal Ministries in Ann Arbor, Michigan. Franciscan University of Steubenville was emerging as a center of sound, orthodox Catholic teaching and spiritual renewal under the leadership of Fr. Michael Scanlan, TOR. There were also a myriad of renewal centers and other ministries and outreaches that were explicitly charismatic or closely related to the Renewal, including new religious and priests' communities and support groups.

What did the new pope, John Paul II, have to say about the Charismatic Renewal? From the beginning of his pontificate, St. John Paul II affirmed the teaching of the Second Vatican Council and announced his firm intention to implement faithfully the teaching of this "council of renewal." As we shall see shortly, the teaching of Vatican II was, along with Sacred Scripture, St. John Paul II's primary source and reference point for whatever he taught on the Holy Spirit and the Renewal.[14]

When St. John Paul first met with Renewal leaders on December 11, 1979, he surprised them by telling them, "I have always belonged to this renewal in the Holy Spirit," and went on "to explain [his] own charismatic life." He recounted how his father had asked him, when he was twelve or thirteen, to

---

14. Pope St. John Paul II has been the "guiding light" for my life and career as a theologian. I started teaching at Franciscan University of Steubenville in January 1978, the year he was elected pope. His teaching inspired me to write a series on his encyclicals for the international catechetical journal *The Sower*, which has been published as a book, *The Legacy of Pope John Paul II* (Steubenville, OH: Emmaus Road, 2006). I also did a miniseries on Pope John Paul II for EWTN.

say a prayer to the Holy Spirit every day of his life. The pope said, "I have remained obedient to this order that my father gave me nearly 50 years ago."[15] Pope St. John Paul II saw himself as *belonging* to this renewal in the Holy Spirit because he *prayed to the Holy Spirit daily.* As a result, the Holy Father went on to say, "I can understand all the different charisms. All of them are part of the riches of the Lord."[16]

In his first apostolic exhortation, *Catechesi Tradendae* [On Catechesis in Our Time], promulgated on October 16, 1979, the Holy Father quoted and affirmed Pope Paul VI's words from *Evangelii Nuntiandi*: "We live in the Church at a privileged moment of the Spirit" (*Catechesi Tradendae,* 72). Popes Paul VI and John Paul II saw that this "privileged moment" of the outpouring of the Holy Spirit was essential for the reawakening of both evangelistic fervor and vibrant catechesis in the Church. New programs or methods cannot substitute for the action of the Holy Spirit. Hence, Pope St. John Paul II followed his predecessor in encouraging the growth of the Renewal.

It is also true that this saintly pope perceived and warned against excesses and dangers in the movement. In a 1980 address to the Italian Renewal, amidst many positive comments, Pope John Paul II warned about risks such as giving too much weight to emotional experience, as well as "unrestrained pursuit of the spectacular and extraordinary" and tolerance of "hasty and distorted interpretations of Scripture."[17] But on May 7,

15. McDonnell, *Open the Windows*, 25–26.

16. Ibid.

17. Ibid., 32.

1981, addressing six hundred delegates of the Renewal from almost one hundred countries, the Holy Father said,

> The church has seen the fruits of your devotion to prayer in a deepened commitment to holiness of life and love for the word of God. We have noted with particular joy the way in which leaders of the renewal have more and more developed a broadened ecclesial vision, and have made efforts to make this vision increasingly a reality for those who depend on them for guidance. We have likewise seen the signs of your generosity in sharing God's gifts with the unfortunate of this world in justice and charity, so that all people may experience the priceless dignity that is theirs in Christ. May this work of love already begun in you be brought to successful completion (cf. 2 Corinthians 8:6, 11)![18]

Pope John Paul II exhorted leaders to (1) "give the example of prayer" and participate in the Church's sacramental and liturgical life; (2) give people "solid food for spiritual nourishment" by teaching true doctrine; and (3) "take the initiative in building bonds of trust and cooperation with the bishops."[19] He also urged them to work with other Christians in seeking Christian unity.

The impact of Pope John Paul II's pontificate on the Renewal cannot be understood only through statements or meetings with charismatic groups and leaders. In his twenty-six plus years as

18. Ibid., 36–37.

19. Ibid., 37–39.

pope, John Paul II presented very comprehensive catecheses on many subjects, including the Holy Spirit. These were based primarily on Sacred Scripture but also drew from Sacred Tradition and were always presented in light of the teachings of the Second Vatican Council.

Not only did St. John Paul write one of his fourteen encyclicals on the Holy Spirit (*Dominum et Vivificantem* [Lord and Giver of Life]), issued on Pentecost 1986, but he also did a thorough, biblically based, systematic catechesis on the Holy Spirit in his Wednesday audiences and on other occasions.[20] In this catechesis he explained the importance and the role of the charisms in Christian life, especially in equipping the laity

20. See over four hundred pages of catechesis on the Holy Spirit presented by Pope St. John Paul II from general audiences given from April 26, 1989, to July 3, 1991, in *The Spirit: Giver of Life and Love: A Catechesis on the Creed,* Vol. 3 (Boston, MA: Pauline Books, 1996). For an even more comprehensive collection, see *The Holy Spirit in the Writings of Pope John Paul II* by Fr. Bill McCarthy, MSA (McKees Rock, PA: St. Andrews Publications, 2001).

for prayer, ministry, and service.[21]

1998 was a climactic year in the pope's teaching on the Holy Spirit and in his recognition of the importance of movements in the Church that he called "charismatic." In preparation for the Great Jubilee of the Year 2000, Pope St. John Paul designated the three preceding years for reflection on the three Persons of the Blessed Trinity, with 1998 being the "Year of the Holy Spirit." As part of that celebration, the Holy Father invited members of all the new ecclesial groups and movements to celebrate Pentecost with him in Rome. It turned out to be the largest such religious gathering of Catholics in Rome in the history of the Catholic Church. What was even more striking

---

21. See the following general audiences by John Paul II: February 27, 1991, http://w2.vatican.va/content/john-paul-ii/es/audiences/1991/documents/hf_jp-ii_aud_19910227.html; June 24, 1992, http://w2.vatican.va/content/john-paul-ii/es/audiences/1992/documents/hf_jp-ii_aud_19920624.html; March 9, 1994, http://w2.vatican.va/content/john-paul-ii/es/audiences/1994/documents/hf_jp-ii_aud_19940309.html; and September 21, 1994, http://w2.vatican.va/content/john-paul-ii/es/audiences/1994/documents/hf_jp-ii_aud_19940921.html. In this last audience, Pope John Paul II remarked, "It is possible to speak of a new lay life, rich in immense human potential, as fact. The true value of this life comes from the Holy Spirit, who abundantly bestows his gifts on the Church, as he has done since the beginning on the day of Pentecost (cf. Acts 2:3-4; 1 Corinthians 12:7ff). In our day too, many signs and great witness have been given by individuals, groups and movements generously dedicated to the apostolate. They show that the marvels of Pentecost have not ceased, but are renewed abundantly in the Church today. It is obvious that in addition to a considerable development in the doctrine of the charisms, there has also been a new flowering of active laypeople in the Church. It is not by chance that the two facts have occurred at the same time. It is all the work of the Holy Spirit, the effective and vital source of everything in the Christian life that is really and authentically evangelical." (McCarthy, *The Holy Spirit in the Writings of Pope John Paul II*, 405)

is what Pope John Paul II said in his Pentecost address to this vast assembly. Citing *Lumen Gentium*, he said that during Vatican II, "the Church rediscovered the charismatic dimension as one of her constitutive elements," adding,

> The institutional and charismatic aspects are co-essential as it were to the Church's constitution. They contribute, although differently, to the life, renewal and sanctification of God's People. It is from this providential rediscovery of the Church's charismatic dimension that, before and after the Council, a remarkable pattern of growth has been established for ecclesial movements and new communities.
>
> Today the Church rejoices at the renewed confirmation of the prophet Joel's words which we have just heard: "I will pour out my Spirit upon all flesh" (Acts 2:17). You, present here, are the tangible proof of this "outpouring" of the Spirit.
>
> Today, I would like to cry out to all of you gathered here in St. Peter's Square and to all Christians: Open yourselves docilely to the gifts of the Spirit! Accept gratefully and obediently the charisms which the Spirit never ceases to bestow on us! Do not forget that every charism is given for the common good, that is, for the benefit of the whole Church.[22]

It is significant that John Paul states that the Catholic Church has "rediscovered the charismatic dimension as one of her constitutive elements" and that the institutional and charismatic

---

22. "This Is the Day the Lord Has Made!" *L'Osservatore Romano*, English edition, No. 22, June 3, 1998, 2.

aspects of the Church are "co-essential." The pope clarifies what is implied but not explicitly stated in the Vatican II documents.

Yet the impact of this event in the life and history of the Church was due to the fact that half a million people, primarily laypeople from the Renewal and many new ecclesial communities, demonstrated the truth and the significance of the pope's words. Indeed, he himself declared, "You, present here, are the tangible proof of this 'outpouring' of the Spirit."

Also in this address, the pope challenged the Renewal and all the gathered movements and communities to enter into a new stage of their life, which he termed "that of ecclesial maturity. . . . The Church expects from you the 'mature' fruits of communion and commitment."[23]

Pope Benedict XVI and the Renewal

The next successor of St. Peter to be elected was the German theologian-turned-bishop and cardinal, Joseph Ratzinger, who took the papal name Benedict XVI. Ratzinger was a theological advisor at the Second Vatican Council, and it was the German bishops who suggested many of the changes brought about by Vatican II.

At that time, Joseph Ratzinger was an up-and-coming young theologian whose thought was being shaped by interaction with other major Catholic theologians, such as his fellow German, Karl Rahner, SJ, who was also a council advisor. In 1969 Rahner published an article that explored the relationship between the

---

23. Ibid.

charismatic and institutional aspects of the Church. He affirmed the teaching of Vatican II that charisms constitute an essential part of the Church; Rahner explained that whereas the institutional aspect of the Church is characterized by stability and thus preserves continuity, "the charismatic manifests itself in ever fresh and unexpected forms, and hence . . . needs to be discovered ever anew."[24] Although God has established the stable sacramental and hierarchical aspects of the Church, God is sovereign over it and can break into the life of the Church whenever and however he wishes. This freedom of God—of the Holy Spirit—represents the charismatic aspect or dimension of the Church. As St. John's Gospel says, "The wind blows where it wills . . . ; so it is with every one who is born of the Spirit" (3:8)[25] As we will see shortly, as cardinal and later as pope, Joseph Ratzinger followed and developed Karl Rahner's line of thought.

We will look at Ratzinger's view of the Renewal beginning with the 1985 book, *The Ratzinger Report*. Cardinal Ratzinger observed that every truly successful ecumenical council in the Church's history was followed by "a wave of holiness." One hopeful sign following Vatican II, he said, was "the rise of new movements which nobody had planned and which nobody called into being." In describing what was happening in the Church after the council, he described it as "something like

---

24. Karl Rahner, "Observations on the Factor of the Charismatic in the Church," in *Theological Investigations, Vol. 12*, trans. David Bourke (New York: Seabury Press, 1974), 84.

25. Ibid., 88–89. Rahner explains that the Church is an "open system"—open to the free and direct action of the Holy Spirit—rather than a "closed system," in which God cannot intervene.

a pentecostal season in the Church. I am thinking, say, of the charismatic movement [and some other movements]."[26] These movements, he said, are marked by loyalty to the Church and her faith, "an intense life of prayer," and "the joy of the faith that . . . has something contagious about it."[27] They are also producing vocations to the priesthood and religious life, as well as active lay involvement in the mission of the Church. How is the Catholic Church to look upon these movements? Cardinal Ratzinger said, "What is emerging here is a new generation of the Church which I am watching with a great hope. I find it marvelous that the Spirit is once more stronger than our programs and brings himself into play in an altogether different way than we had imagined."[28]

The cardinal was open to the surprises of the Holy Spirit! How was the hierarchy of the Church to respond to these new movements? "Our task—the task of the officeholders in the Church and of theologians—is to keep the door open to them, to prepare room for them."[29]

Toward the end of this same book, the interviewer asked Cardinal Ratzinger specifically about the Renewal. The cardinal said that it was a response to Pope John XXIII's prayer for a "new Pentecost."

---

26. Joseph Cardinal Ratzinger with Vittorio Messori, *The Ratzinger Report: An Exclusive Interview on the State of the Church*, trans. Salvator Attanasio and Graham Harrison (San Francisco, CA: Ignatius Press, 1985), 43.

27. Ibid.

28. Ibid., 44.

29. Ibid.

"In the heart of a world desiccated by rationalistic scepticism a new experience of the Holy Spirit has come about, amounting to a worldwide renewal movement. What the New Testament describes, with reference to the charisms, as visible signs of the coming of the Spirit is no longer merely ancient, past history: this history is becoming a burning reality today."

"It is no accident," he stresses, in support of his view of the Spirit as the antithesis of the demonic, "that whereas a reductionist theology treats the devil and the world of evil spirits as a mere label, there is in the 'Renewal' a new and concrete awareness of the powers of evil in addition, of course, to the calm certainty of the power of Christ who subjugates them all."[30]

In response to the interviewer's question regarding the risks or dangers of the Renewal, Cardinal Ratzinger responded with a standard list whose elements had been included in statements of many bishops' conferences: the possibility of "an exclusive emphasis on the Spirit"; seeing the "charismatic" church and "freedom of the Spirit" as in opposition to the hierarchically structured church; placing personal experience above or in opposition to doctrine; a "too-easy ecumenism" that could succumb to fundamentalism; and failure or hesitation to act in unity with bishops and priests.[31] In spite of these risks and dangers, Cardinal Ratzinger concluded that the Renewal is "a

---

30. Ibid., 151.

31. Ibid., 152.

gift of God to our age."[32]

Let's fast-forward thirteen years, to May 27–29, 1998. Immediately preceding Pope St. John Paul II's Pentecost Mass, there was a World Congress of Ecclesial Movements that addressed what the Holy Spirit was saying and doing through these new movements, the Charismatic Renewal being the largest of them worldwide. Cardinal Ratzinger opened this congress with a masterful speech on the place of ecclesial movements in the Church. He began with an excerpt from Pope John Paul II's encyclical *Redemptoris Missio* [Mission of the Redeemer], which expressed delight in "the rapid growth of 'ecclesial movements' filled with missionary dynamism" (72). Cardinal Ratzinger referred to Karl Rahner's observation that after the hopeful beginnings of implementing Vatican II, in the early 1970s a "winter of fatigue" and discouragement had slowly crept into the Church. "But then something suddenly happened which no one had planned. The Holy Spirit had, so to say, once again made his voice heard. The faith was reawakened, especially in young people."[33]

---

32. Ibid., 153. The full statement reads: "It is evidence of hope, a positive sign of the times, a gift of God to our age. It is a rediscovery of the joy and wealth of prayer over against theories and practices which had become increasingly ossified and shriveled as a result of secularized rationalism. I myself have observed the effectiveness of the Movement: in Munich I saw a number of good vocations to the priesthood come from it. As I have already said, like every other reality entrusted to human beings, it too is exposed to misunderstandings, misinterpretations and exaggeration. But it would be dangerous to see only the risks and not also the gift offered by God. The necessary caution does not alter my fundamentally positive judgment."

33. Ratzinger, "The Ecclesial Movements," 24.

In this remarkable address, Cardinal Ratzinger once again affirmed that the Renewal and other new ecclesial movements were the result of an "irruption of the Holy Spirit." Nonetheless, these movements "had their share of childhood diseases," especially an exclusivity in which members of these movements were sometimes critical of the lack of fervor in the "local Church" and expected it "to crank itself up to their level, to adapt itself to their form, and not vice versa. . . . Frictions arose, at which both sides were at fault in different ways." Cardinal Ratzinger noted that this challenge of properly integrating new movements, "new irruptions of the Holy Spirit, which continually revitalize and renew that structure," into the life of the Church was not anything new. Such a challenge and task is actually a blessing to the Church, reminding us that the charismatic dimension of the Church (which, after all, was born at Pentecost) precedes and is the basis of the Church as a hierarchical institution. Considering this, Cardinal Ratzinger made the rather bold statement that local churches and even the bishops "must avoid any uniformity of pastoral organizations and programs." He continued,

> They must not turn their own pastoral plans into the criterion of what the Holy Spirit is allowed to do: an obsession with planning could render the Churches impervious to the action of the Holy Spirit, to the power of God by which they live. Not everything should be fitted into the straightjacket of a single uniform organization; what is needed is less organization and more spirit![34]

---

34. Ibid., 50.

The cardinal even asserted that any concept of *communio* in the Church that means simply avoiding conflict is false, because "faith remains a sword and may demand conflict for the sake of truth and love (cf. Matthew 10:34)."[35]

He also warned against labeling "the zeal of those seized by the Holy Spirit and their uninhibited faith with the anathema of fundamentalism," reaffirming his point that the Church needs "less organization and more spirit." With regard to the priesthood, he said,

> It is important that the sacred ministry, the priesthood itself, be charismatically understood and lived. The priest himself should be a "pneumatic," a *homo spiritualis*, a man aroused and impelled by the Holy Spirit. It is the Church's task to make sure that this character of the sacrament be seen and accepted. . . . And she must do everything she can to help those called to the priesthood to preserve their faith beyond the initial enthusiasm, and not get slowly bogged down in routine. She must help them increasingly to become truly spiritual men.
>
> Where the sacred ministry is lived pneumatically and charismatically in this way, no institutional hardening takes place: what exists, instead, is an inner responsiveness to the charism, a kind of instinct for the Holy Spirit and his action. And so the charism too can once again recognize its own origin in the holder of the ministry, and ways will be found for fruitful collaboration in the discernment of spirits.[36]

---

35. Ibid.

36. Ibid., 28–29.

I quote this address at length to dispel the image of Cardinal Ratzinger (and later, Pope Benedict XVI) as a leader who sought to maintain or defend a certain formalism, rubrism, or traditionalism in the Catholic Church, set in opposition to the Renewal or other new ecclesial movements and groups. This is simply not the case. His statements and actions as pope bear this out. Pope Benedict XVI's meetings with leaders of the Italian and international Renewal were cordial and supportive, and he expressed his desire to foster a "culture of Pentecost" in the Catholic Church.[37] Actually, that phrase was first used by Pope St. John Paul II, who said,

> In our time that is so hungry for hope, make the Holy Spirit known and loved. Help bring to life that "culture of Pentecost" that alone can make fruitful the civilization of love and friendly co-existence among peoples. With fervent insistence, never tire of praying, "Come Holy Spirit! Come! Come!"[38]

Following the example of his beloved and respected predecessor, Pope St. John Paul II, Pope Benedict XVI invited members of the new ecclesial movements to celebrate Pentecost with him

---

37. Benedict XVI, Address to Participants in the Meeting Sponsored by "Renewal in the Holy Spirit," May 26, 2012, http://w2.vatican.va/content/benedict-xvi/en/speeches/2012/may/documents/hf_ben-xvi_spe_20120526_rinnov-spirito.html.

38. John Paul II, Address to a Delegation of Members of the Renewal in the Holy Spirit Movement, March 14, 2002, http://w2.vatican.va/content/john-paul-ii/en/speeches/2002/march/documents/hf_jp-ii_spe_20020314_rinnovamento-spirito-santo.html.

in Rome in 2006, as Pope John Paul II had done in that historic inaugural gathering in 1998. An estimated 350,000 people gathered with Pope Benedict in St. Peter's Square on June 3-4, 2006. He emphasized that the Holy Spirit brings us life and freedom.[39]

If one were to take a single year of Pope Benedict XVI's pontificate to measure his emphasis on the Holy Spirit, his addresses of 2008 would be "off the charts." His theme for the 2008 World Youth Day in Australia was Acts 1:8: "You will receive power when the Holy Spirit has come upon you; and you will be my witnesses" (NRSV). At New York's St. Patrick's Cathedral during his papal visit to the United States that same year, Pope Benedict prayed, "Let us implore from God the grace of a new Pentecost for the Church in America. May tongues of fire, combining burning love of God and neighbor with zeal for the spread of Christ's Kingdom, descend on all present!" He spoke three times of the gifts of the Spirit, referencing St. Paul's definition of charisms: "manifestations of the Spirit given for the good of all" (see 1 Corinthians 12:7). Mentioning the Holy Spirit sixteen times in his homily, he ended with the wish that "the Church of America will know a new springtime in the Spirit."[40] Two days earlier in Nationals Stadium in Washington, D.C., the pope proclaimed,

39. Benedict XVI, Meeting with the Ecclesial Movements and New Communities, June 3, 2006, http://w2.vatican.va/content/benedict-xvi/en/homilies/2006/documents/hf_ben-xvi_hom_20060603_veglia-pentecoste.html.

40. Benedict XVI, Homily, April 19, 2008, http://w2.vatican.va/content/benedict-xvi/en/homilies/2008/documents/hf_ben-xvi_hom_20080419_st-patrick-ny.html.

I have come to repeat the Apostle's urgent call to conversion and the forgiveness of sins, and to implore from the Lord a new outpouring of the Holy Spirit upon the Church in this country. . . . Pray that the Holy Spirit will pour out his gifts upon the Church, the gifts that lead to conversion, forgiveness and growth in holiness.[41]

Isn't it significant that in two of his major homilies in the United States, Pope Benedict should have focused so much on the Holy Spirit and called for prayer for a "new Pentecost" and a "new springtime in the Spirit" in this country? (Have American Catholics done this?)

One final teaching of Pope Benedict XVI, also from 2008, was his Regina Caeli address on Pentecost Sunday. He noted that Pentecost is "the Baptism of the Church." He continued,

In this Baptism of the Holy Spirit the personal and the communal dimension, the "I" of the disciple and the "we" of the Church, are inseparable. The Holy Spirit consecrates the person and at the same time makes him or her a living member of the Mystical Body of Christ, sharing in the mission of witnessing to his love. And this takes place through the Sacraments of Christian initiation: Baptism and Confirmation. In my Message for the next World Youth Day 2008, I have proposed to the young people that they rediscover the

---

41. Benedict XVI, Homily, April 17, 2008, http://w2.vatican.va/content/benedict-xvi/en/homilies/2008/documents/hf_ben-xvi_hom_20080417_washington-stadium.html.

Holy Spirit's presence in their lives and thus the importance of these Sacraments. Today I would like to extend the invitation to all: let us rediscover, dear brothers and sisters, the beauty of being baptized in the Holy Spirit; let us recover awareness of our Baptism and our Confirmation, ever timely sources of grace.[42]

These oft-quoted words of Pope Benedict, "Let us rediscover, dear brothers and sisters, the beauty of being baptized in the Holy Spirit," correspond perfectly with the mainstream pastoral and theological understanding of what the Renewal calls being "baptized in the Holy Spirit." It is a personal rediscovery and renewal of the Holy Spirit, who is given to each baptized and confirmed person. It can also be the sending of the Holy Spirit to an unbaptized person, as we see in Acts 10:25-48 when Peter preached to Cornelius, but that account also shows that the gift of the Spirit in such a case must lead to water baptism and is intrinsically connected to it.

When Pope Benedict prayed for a "new Pentecost" or "a new springtime of the Spirit," he was referring to this same fresh outpouring of the Holy Spirit that is the hallmark and primary apostolate of the Renewal whose anniversary we celebrate.

---

42. Benedict XVI, Regina Caeli, May 11, 2008, http://w2.vatican.va/content/benedict-xvi/en/angelus/2008/documents/hf_ben-xvi_reg_20080511_pentecoste.html.

Other Pastoral Statements from the
Catholic Hierarchy

Besides these papal teachings and addresses concerning the Holy
Spirit and the Renewal, there also have been other constitu-
encies in the Catholic Church's hierarchy who have provided
pastoral reflection on or guidance for the Renewal. They are
too numerous even for a bibliography in this work, but I will
conclude this chapter with two examples: pastoral statements
of the United States Catholic bishops and a recent letter to
all bishops from the Sacred Congregation for the Doctrine of
the Faith.

I have already mentioned the short but positive early statement on the "Pentecostal Movement in the Catholic Church"
issued by the Committee on Doctrine of the (U.S.) National
Conference of Catholic Bishops on November 14, 1969. Two
further statements were issued by the Catholic bishops of the
United States. The first was prepared by the Committee on
Pastoral Research and Practices in 1975. The Renewal had
grown rapidly in the United States between 1969 and 1975,
and of course, some questions—and problems—had arisen
that required a pastoral response from the Church. The 1975
statement was divided into fifteen points, with an address by
Pope Paul VI from October 16, 1974, appended to it.[43]

It is fascinating to read a pastoral statement written only
eight years after the emergence of the Renewal by a committee

---

43. This statement is found in McDonnell, *Presence, Power, Praise, Vol. II,*
104–111.

who was familiar with the teaching of Scripture and Vatican II but had little firsthand experience of the Renewal. The tone is quite cautionary. Regarding the charisms, it warns of "the possibility of self-deception" and states "such things as healing, prophecy, praying in tongues, and the interpretation of tongues . . . call for caution . . . and their importance, even if genuine, should not be exaggerated."[44] (Those who had been healed, touched by a prophetic word, or who had found a new freedom to praise God in tongues might find this warning difficult to understand.) The following criteria were presented for discerning "such gifts as tongues, miracles, or prophecies": (1) "conformity with the full teaching of the Gospel and the following of [Jesus'] example"; (2) that these "gifts of the Spirit build up the Church in unity and charity"; (3) that they be exercised in love ("the greatest authenticating sign of the Spirit"); (4) that "the Spirit always bears witness to Jesus"; and (5) that their use never conflicts with official Church teaching, and is guided by the wisdom of the Church's saints and spiritual masters.[45]

These are all sound principles, and the bottom line is that when they are followed, there are no other restrictions or limitations placed on the exercise of charisms in the Renewal.

Also emphasized was the need for those in the Renewal to remain involved in their parish community and to seek the guidance of parish priests. Priests are "strongly encouraged . . . to take an interest in the movement." Priests who are not

44. Ibid., 109.

45. Ibid., 107–108.

personally involved in the movement should "be cautious in making judgments or decisions and should make sure they are fully informed and understand what is taking place."[46]

The bishops stressed the need for good communication between Renewal leaders and the pastors and bishops as well as the need for formation of Renewal leaders, saying the "less mature persons" should be under the direction "of the more mature." There was a concern that charismatic groups that were ecumenical might run the risk of diluting the Catholic identity of Catholic members, and there were warnings against elitism and fundamentalism. Small communities must follow these norms, foster mature leadership, and maintain "a strong link with the ecclesial community."[47]

There is one paragraph (5) that focuses on the "positive signs" of the movement: faith in Christ, renewed interest in prayer, "heightened consciousness of the action of the Holy Spirit, the praise of God," and deepened personal commitment to Jesus Christ, and, for many, growth in devotion to the Eucharist, love of Mary, and greater participation in the Church's sacramental life.[48] The statement ends on a positive note: "We encourage those who already belong and we support the positive and desirable directions of the charismatic renewal."[49]

Nine years later, another "Pastoral Statement on the Catholic

---

46. Ibid., 110.

47. Ibid., 110–111.

48. Ibid., 108.

49. Ibid., 111.

Charismatic Renewal" was issued to update the 1975 statement.[50] The committee that issued this statement was made up of seven bishops who were involved in or favorable to the Renewal, with Fr. Kilian McDonnell, OSB, as a consultant. The statement was divided into two parts and a conclusion.

As a document written by bishops and addressed to fellow bishops, the purpose of Part I, entitled "Pastoral Observations," is to call attention to the strengths and positive contributions of the Renewal to the Church, and so it begins by noting the support of both Pope Paul VI and Pope John Paul II for the Renewal. It then enumerates several strengths of the Renewal, including fostering a personal relationship with God, openness to the Holy Spirit and the spiritual gifts (charisms), promoting an active laity who use their charisms to minister to others, renewal of the family, and advocating strong Christian relationships and community (both prayer groups and covenant communities). The bishops are encouraged to assign a diocesan liaison who is familiar with the Renewal and respected by its participants.[51]

While the "forms" of the charismatic movement, such as prayer groups, conferences, or publications, are "optional," the statement stressed that the central concerns of the Renewal—"the covenant love of the Father, the Lordship of Jesus, the power of the Spirit, sacramental and community life, prayer, charisms, and the necessity of evangelization"—are

---

50. Subtitled "A Statement of the Bishops' Liaison Committee with the Catholic Charismatic Renewal," (Washington, D.C.: United States Catholic Conference, 1984). Publication No. 931.

51. Ibid., 4–9.

all a necessary part of Christian life. Therefore, the Renewal "cannot be dismissed as peripheral to the life of the Church. Clearly the charismatic renewal is in and for the Church, not alongside the Church."[52]

The second part of the statement, "Pastoral Orientations," presents elements of the Renewal that either can contribute to the life of the Church, require some development and pastoral guidance, or both. These areas are the focus on evangelization; the need for concrete expression of social concern; the value of formation programs such as Life in the Spirit seminars; the challenge of those who have left or are considering leaving the Catholic Church; proper expression and guidance of ecumenism; healing and deliverance ministries; the threat of fundamentalism (which is not limited to the Renewal); and striking the balance, especially in covenant communities, between accountability and "overcontrol."[53] It is noteworthy that the document states this:

> To a great extent the success of the renewal depends on an informed, balanced, mature, doctrinally sound leadership, especially at the local and diocesan levels. . . . In smaller prayer groups with fewer numbers and smaller resources, the lack of leadership [or well-formed leadership] can be acute.[54]

---

52. Ibid., 4.

53. Ibid., 11–18.

54. Ibid., 17.

Even though this pastoral statement was written over thirty years ago, much of it still remains relevant. Particularly in the United States, we have witnessed the decline and disappearance of many small charismatic prayer groups in homes and parishes that were flourishing in the 1970s and 1980s. The decline is due, in part, to the lack of stable leadership. Many who led prayer groups for many years finally were burned out, causing the groups to fold. Conferences, speakers, and periodicals in the Renewal increasingly began to call for a "renewal of the Renewal" or, biblically speaking, a return to "the love you had at first" (Revelation 2:4) or a rekindling of the gift of God (cf. 2 Timothy 1:6). But we will return to this in the next two chapters.

In sum, advocacy and guidance for the Renewal by popes, bishops, and clergy (as well as religious) over the past fifty years have not been lacking. The thorny theological issue of the relationship between the charismatic and hierarchical/institutional dimensions of the Church has been discussed and largely resolved. This is not to be taken for granted, because the Charismatic Renewal/Pentecostal movement has not met with the same acceptance in the mainline Protestant and Orthodox world as it has in the Catholic Church. This was due to the difficulty of working out the way in which the Charismatic Renewal (especially certain charisms and baptism in the Holy Spirit) could be understood and properly integrated into an established church structure or hierarchy.

The Letter *Iuvenescit Ecclesia*

The Congregation for the Doctrine of the Faith published a letter, *Iuvenescit Ecclesia* [The Church Rejuvenates], on May 14, 2016.[55] This document confirms and summarizes what the Catholic Church has been teaching since Vatican II about the charismatic dimension of the Church and the "co-essentiality" of the charisms and the sacraments, as Pope St. John Paul II also taught. "The Paraclete is, contemporaneously, the one who distributes efficaciously, through the sacraments, the salvific grace offered by Christ . . . and He is the one who bestows the charisms" (*Iuvenescit Ecclesia*, 12).

Even though most of what is said about the charisms in this letter is taken directly from Vatican II and papal documents (especially Pope St. John Paul II and Pope Francis), the way that the letter frequently accentuates the importance of the charisms is striking. The charisms, as Vatican II says, "are not to be considered optional in the life of the Church"; each believer has the right and the duty to use them for the good of the Church and in the freedom of the Holy Spirit. The letter continues, "The authentic charisms, therefore, come to be considered as gifts of indispensable importance for the life and mission of the Church" (9). One reason they are of such importance is that they enable each person in the Church to minister and serve others according to God's gift, thus providing a way that the

55. The Sacred Congregation for the Doctrine of the Faith, *Iuvenescit Ecclesia* [The Church Rejuvenates], May 15, 2016, http://www.vatican.va/roman_curia/congregations/cfaith/documents/ rc_con_cfaith_doc_20160516_iuvenescit-ecclesia_en.html.

grace given through the sacraments can bear fruit in the service of God and neighbor. "The charismatic gifts, therefore, are freely distributed by the Holy Spirit, so that sacramental grace may be fruitful in Christian life in different ways and at every level" (15).

However, one challenge is that the word "charism" has different meanings in Scripture and in common usage in the Catholic Church today. "Charism" may refer to the particular gift the Spirit bestows on an individual (as listed in the New Testament), or it may refer to a particular grace or vision given to a person to begin a movement or a group that continues to live out this "charism of the founder," or it could refer to the grace to live a particular vocation in the Church, such as the consecrated life or the charism of celibacy. This document does not discuss the particular New Testament charisms commonly found in the Renewal and how to discern and pastor them. Rather, it provides pastoral guidelines that will help bishops and pastors integrate "charismatic entities" (groups and movements with distinct visions, missions, and charisms) into the life of the Church in a way that ensures unity and harmony.

Iuvenescit Ecclesia affirms that "the charismatic gifts, when exercised, can generate affinities, closeness, and spiritual relationships." This is certainly true! It continues, "Through these [charismatic gifts] the charismatic patrimony, originating in the person of the founder, is shared in and deepened, thereby giving life to true spiritual families" (16). It is true that in the Renewal, there are prayer groups and communities that were "founded" by a person or persons who influenced the group and perhaps gave their particular "spiritual family" a distinctive vision or mission. However, in a deeper sense, as we have seen, the Renewal has no human founder. Jesus began sovereignly to baptize Catholics in the Holy Spirit and lavish charisms upon them. Hence, "the charismatic patrimony originating in the person of the founder" in the Renewal is this phenomenon of Jesus and the Father pouring out the Holy Spirit in a new way among Catholics, with the full range of charisms listed in the New Testament being manifested in the way St. Paul described, giving gifts "to each . . . for the common good" (1 Corinthians 12:7).[56]

How, according to the guidelines and teaching of *Iuvenescit Ecclesia,* is this massive worldwide "charismatic entity"—the Renewal—to be integrated harmoniously into the sacramental and hierarchical dimensions of the Catholic Church? We will explore this question in the next two chapters. We will also complete the discussion of what Catholic ecclesial leaders have to say about the Renewal by looking at the teachings of Pope Francis and of the preacher of the papal household under three popes, Fr. Raniero Cantalamessa, OFM, Cap.

---

56. Some of the charisms of the Renewal are listed in *Iuvenescit Ecclesia,* 18: "Presence of spiritual fruits such as charity, joy, peace and a certain human maturity (cf. Gal 5:22); the desire 'to live the Church's life more intensely,' a more intense desire of 'listening to and meditating on the Word'; 'the renewed appreciation for prayer, contemplation, liturgical and sacramental life, the reawakening of vocations to Christian marriage, the ministerial priesthood and the consecrated life.'"

Chapter 7

Pope Francis and the Renewal

Where is the Renewal today? Where is it going tomorrow? As we have seen, the Catholic Charismatic Renewal has flourished and been blessed, not only by the grace of God, which is primary, but also because of the human response to this outpouring of the Holy Spirit. This includes the many faithful participants and leaders within the Renewal as well as the support of the leaders in the Catholic hierarchy who have been open to the action of the Holy Spirit in our time and have provided pastoral guidance for the Renewal's sound development.

Though I have focused on the teachings and guidance of recent popes and bishops' conferences, I would be remiss if I did not also gratefully acknowledge the work of the Pontifical Council for the Laity. Prefects of this Vatican office, notably Archbishops Paul Cordes and Stanislaw Ryłko, have worked closely with Renewal leaders over the course of many years, cultivating the seeds of renewal in a way that has enabled these leaders to grow and to mature.

In evaluating where the Renewal is today and how it might develop in the future, let's begin with the teaching and vision of the current pope at this writing, Pope Francis, and the preacher most widely recognized in the Renewal and most highly respected by the Catholic hierarchy, Fr. Raniero Cantalamessa, OFM Cap.

Pope Francis' Relationship with the Renewal

In assessing Pope Francis' relationship to the Renewal, we cannot forget that he comes from a part of the world, Latin America, where Pentecostalism has converted many baptized Catholics.[1] One antidote or answer to this situation has been the growth of the Catholic Charismatic Renewal in the region. However, Pope Francis admits that his reaction to the Renewal in the late seventies and early eighties was negative. "These people confuse a liturgical celebration with samba lessons," he admitted to having once said.[2]

Pope Francis' evaluation of the Renewal has changed radically since those days. Returning from World Youth Day in Rio in 2013, Pope Francis said, "I don't think that the charismatic renewal movement merely prevents people from passing over to Pentecostal denominations. No! It is also a service to the church herself! It renews us."[3]

Pope Francis seems to have taken a particular pastoral interest in the Renewal. He understands the movement well, both its strengths and weaknesses, as if from the "inside." In an address to the 37th National (Italian) Convocation of the

---

1. For example, "A 2006 Pew Research Center survey of Pentecostals in Brazil found that 45 percent were converts from Catholicism." Francis X. Rocca, "Pope Francis discovers charismatic movement a gift to the whole church," Catholic News Service, August 9, 2013, http://www.catholicnews.com/services/englishnews/2013/pope-francis-discovers-charismatic-movement-a-gift-to-the-whole-church.cfm.

2. Ibid.

3. Ibid.

Renewal in the Holy Spirit, he compared the Church, and charismatics in particular, to a "great orchestra, where all the instruments and voices are different from one another, yet all are needed to create the harmony of the music." This analogy, he explained, is based on St. Paul's teaching in 1 Corinthians 12, which emphasizes that each person in the Church has a particular charism (sometimes more than one), and all are important for the Church. When the Holy Father got the crowd involved by asking, "Who is the head of the Renewal?" the answer, which the pope affirmed, was "The Lord Jesus!"

At this gathering Pope Francis told the story of how he had turned from a skeptic to a supporter of the Renewal.

> I didn't share their style of prayer or the many new things which were happening in the Church. Later, I got to know them and I finally realized all the good that the charismatic renewal was doing for the Church. And this story which began with the "samba school" had an unexpected ending: a few months before entering the conclave, I was named the spiritual assistant for the charismatic renewal in Argentina by the Conference of Bishops.
>
> The charismatic renewal is a great force meant to serve the preaching of the Gospel in the joy of the Holy Spirit.[4]

---

4. Francis, Address to Participants in the 37th National Convocation of the Renewal in the Holy Spirit, June 1, 2014, http://w2.vatican.va/content/francesco/en/speeches/2014/june/documents/papa-francesco_20140601_rinnovamento-spirito-santo.html.

This theme of "preaching the Gospel in the joy of the Holy Spirit" is evidently very close to Pope Francis' heart. His first apostolic exhortation, *Evangelii Gaudium* [The Joy of the Gospel], issued on November 24, 2013, concludes with a chapter entitled "Spirit-Filled Evangelizers":

> Spirit-filled evangelizers means evangelizers fearlessly open to the working of the Holy Spirit. At Pentecost, the Spirit made the apostles go forth from themselves and turned them into heralds of God's wondrous deeds, capable of speaking to each person in his or her own language. The Holy Spirit also grants the courage to proclaim the newness of the Gospel with boldness (*parrhesia*) in every time and place, even when it meets with opposition. Let us call upon him today, firmly rooted in prayer, for without prayer all our activity risks being fruitless and our message empty. Jesus wants evangelizers who proclaim the good news not only with words, but above all by a life transfigured by God's presence. (259)

Ever since Pope St. John Paul II began to speak about a new evangelization in the early 1980s, there has been much study and discussion of the subject. But no one has figured out how to motivate the average Catholic in the pew to begin proclaiming "the newness of the Gospel with boldness (*parrhesia*)." Pope Francis understands that the only solution is a new outpouring of the Holy Spirit, as he goes on to explain in *Evangelii Gaudium*:

Spirit-filled evangelization is not the same as a set of tasks dutifully carried out despite one's own personal inclinations and wishes. How I long to find the right words to stir up enthusiasm for a new chapter of evangelization full of fervor, joy, generosity, courage, boundless love and attraction! Yet I realize that no words of encouragement will be enough unless the fire of the Holy Spirit burns in our hearts. A spirit-filled evangelization is one guided by the Holy Spirit, for he is the soul of the Church called to proclaim the Gospel. . . . I once more invoke the Holy Spirit. I implore him to come and renew the Church, to stir and impel her to go forth boldly to evangelize all peoples. (261)

Before Pope Francis' pontificate, at a March 2011 international colloquium of Renewal leaders in Rome, a phrase became popular that anticipated what Pope Francis would say in *Evangelii Gaudium*: "No new evangelization without a new Pentecost." As Pope Francis says, without the fire of the Holy Spirit burning in our hearts, no words of exhortation or encouragement will be sufficient to spark a new wave of true evangelistic fervor.

There are many other themes in Pope Francis' teaching that resonate with the life and experience of those in the Renewal. He frequently remarks that Christians ought to be joyful and that this joy is a fruit of the Holy Spirit.[5] Joy is also a result of praising God, which we need to "rediscover."[6] We must learn to be docile to the Holy Spirit—attentive to his voice and responsive to his promptings. Pope Francis urges this docility, this openness, to the Holy Spirit both in our personal lives, through prayer, and also in the working of the Holy Spirit in the Church.

---

5. For example, in a homily at Santa Marta on May 15, 2015, Pope Francis taught, "Christian joy is not simply enjoyment, is not a fleeting cheerfulness. Christian joy is a gift, it is a gift of the Holy Spirit. And having a heart that is always joyful because the Lord has triumphed, the Lord reigns, the Lord is at the right hand of the Father, the Lord has looked upon me and called me and has given me His grace, and has made me a Son of the Father. . . . That is Christian joy. A Christian lives in joy." "Pope: Fearful and joyless communities are not Christian," Vatican Radio, May 15, 2015, http://en.radiovaticana.va/news/2015/05/15/ pope_fearful_and_joyless_communities_are_not_christian/1144254.

6. On October 16, 2014, Pope Francis said, "We know very well how to pray when we want to ask for things, even when we want to thank the Lord, but a prayer of praise is a bit more difficult for us: we are not used to praising the Lord. We can do this better by remembering all of the things that the Lord has done for us in our lives: 'In Him—in Christ—He chose us before the creation of the world.' Blessed are you, Lord, because You chose me! It is the joy of a paternal and tender closeness." "Prayers of praise"— he continued—bring us this joy, [the joy of] being happy before the Lord. Let's make a real effort to rediscover this!" . . . A prayer of praise, concluded the Pope, is therefore first and foremost a "prayer of joy," then a "prayer of remembrance." "How much the Lord has done for me! How tenderly He has accompanied me, how he has lowered Himself: like a father bows down over a child to help him walk." And finally a prayer to the Holy Spirit that we may receive the grace "to enter into the Mystery, especially when we celebrate the Eucharist." "Pope at Santa Marta: In praise of God," Vatican Radio, October 16, 2014, http://en.radiovaticana.va/news/2014/10/16/ pope_at_santa_marta_in_praise_of_god/1108702.

On the personal level, the pope says that not even a thousand catechism, spirituality, yoga, or Zen courses "will be able to give you the freedom as a child of God. Only the Holy Spirit can prompt your heart to say, 'Father.' Only the Holy Spirit is capable of banishing, of breaking, that hardness of heart and making it . . . 'docile.' Docile towards the Lord. Docile when it comes to the freedom to love."[7]

On the level of the Church, the pope affirms that the Holy Spirit keeps the Church moving forward or, as Pope St. John XXIII said, updates the Church.[8] Yet he warns that we must overcome our resistance to the Holy Spirit's action, our desire

7. "Pope Francis: Only the Holy Spirit opens our hearts to love God," Vatican Radio, January 9, 2015, http://en.radiovaticana.va/news/2015/01/09/pope_francis_only_the_spirit_opens_our_hearts_to_love_god/1117555.

8. "Pope at Mass: The Holy Spirit makes the unthinkable possible," Vatican Radio, May 12, 2014, http://en.radiovaticana.va/storico/2014/05/12/pope_at_mass_the_holy_spirit_makes_the_unthinkable_possible/en1-798509. He concluded: "We Christians must ask the Lord for the grace of docility to the Holy Spirit. Docility in this Spirit, who speaks to us in our heart, who speaks to us in all of life's circumstances, who speaks to us in the Church's life, in Christian communities, who is always speaking to us."

to tame the Holy Spirit when he surprises us or challenges us to change.[9]

Regarding the charisms, we have already noted Pope Francis' image of the Church as a great orchestra in which each person uses his or her own unique charisms to produce a rich and glorious harmony. Pope Francis also builds upon the teaching on the importance of charisms that was emphasized so often by Pope St. John Paul II, which in turn was based upon the teaching of the Second Vatican Council.[10] Pope Francis distinguishes between the popular understanding of "charism" as natural talent or ability and the Christian meaning of "charism" as "a grace, a gift bestowed by God the Father, through the action of the Holy Spirit . . . because with the same freely given love

---

9. Pope Francis has reflected on how the Holy Spirit guides the Church in unity through prayer and dialogue: "The way the Church expresses its communion is through synodality, by meeting, listening, debating, praying and deciding. The Spirit is always the protagonist and the Lord asks us not to be afraid when the Spirit calls us. Just as the Spirit stopped St. Paul and set him on the right road, so the Spirit will give us the courage and the patience to win over adversity and stand firm in the face of martyrdom. Let us ask the Lord for grace, the Pope concluded, to understand how the Church can face the surprises of the Spirit, to be docile and to follow the path which Christ wants for us and for the whole Church." "Pope: There is always resistance in the Church to surprises of the Spirit," Vatican Radio, April 28, 2016, http://en.radiovaticana.va/news/2016/04/28/pope_there_is_always_resistance_to_surprises_of_the_spirit/1226132.

10. See, for example, Pope John Paul II's apostolic exhortation, *Christifideles Laici* [On the Lay Members of Christ's Faithful People], December 30, 1988, 21, 23, 24, http://w2.vatican.va/content/john-paul-ii/en/apost_exhortations/documents/hf_jp-ii_exh_30121988_christifideles-laici.html.

he can place him in service to the entire community, for the good of all."[11]

A person's charisms can only be recognized as such within the Christian community, he says, because charisms are not given as much to individuals as to the Christian community, which benefits from an authentic charism:

> Each one of us should ask him/herself: "Is there a charism that the Lord has endowed me with, by the grace of his Spirit, and that my brothers and sisters in the Christian community have recognized and encouraged? And how do I act with regard to this gift: do I use it with generosity, placing it at the service of everyone, or do I overlook it and end up forgetting about it? Or perhaps it becomes a reason for pride in me, such that I always complain about others and insist on getting my way in the community?

Pope Francis warns, "Never must these gifts become reasons for envy, or for division, for jealousy! . . . Within the Christian community, we need one another, and each gift received is fully realized when it is shared with one's brothers and sisters, for the good of all. This is the Church!" In the same general audience, the Holy Father summarizes his understanding of the charisms:

---

11. Francis, General Audience, October 1, 2014, http://w2.vatican.va/
content/francesco/en/audiences/2014/documents/papa-francesco_20141001_
udienza-generale.html.

The most beautiful experience, though, is the discovery of all the different charisms and all the gifts of his Spirit that the Father showers on his Church! This must not be seen as a reason for confusion, for discomfort: they are all gifts that God gives to the Christian community, in order that it may grow in harmony, in the faith and in his love, as one body, the Body of Christ. The same Spirit who bestows this diversity of charisms unites the Church. It is always the same Spirit.

Considering that this discourse on the charisms was given at a general audience, Pope Francis appears to assume that this "beautiful experience" of discovering, discerning, and using the charisms ought to be a normal and accepted part of Catholic life. Let's return to that assumption later when we assess the acceptance and status of the Renewal in the Catholic Church today.

Pope Francis on Unity in the Spirit

From his actions and teachings, it is clear that working toward the full unity of all Christians is a high priority in Pope Francis' pontificate. He has said that building the unity of the Church "is the task of every Christian." Who builds this unity? "It is the work of the Holy Spirit. The Spirit is the only one capable of building the unity of the Church." But unity within the Church and with other Christians can only be achieved if, like Jesus, we become "weak" with the virtues of humility, generosity, gentleness, meekness, and magnanimity.[12]

The efforts of the popes since the Second Vatican Council to seek and advance unity among Christians have been impressive. Recent popes have visited and reached out to both Orthodox and Protestant leaders, not to mention participating in interreligious meetings. But only Pope Francis has had regular contact and fostered friendships with Pentecostal evangelicals.

---

12. "Pope at Santa Marta: Unity in diversity," Vatican Radio, October 24, 2014, http://en.radiovaticana.va/news/2014/10/24/pope_at_santa_marta_unity_in_diversity/1109323. Pope Francis also reflected on Christian unity and the Holy Spirit's role in bringing this about in a homily given at vespers at the close of the Week of Prayer for Christian Unity in 2015: "From the pierced side of Jesus there flowed blood and water (cf. John 19:34). He is the brimming fount of the water of the Holy Spirit, 'the love of God poured into our hearts' (Romans 5:5) on the day of our baptism. By the working of the Holy Spirit, we have become one in Christ, sons in the Son, true worshipers of the Father. This mystery of love is the deepest ground of the unity which binds all Christians and is much greater than their historical divisions. To the extent that we humbly advance towards the Lord, then, we also draw nearer to one another." Francis, Homily, January 25, 2015, http://w2.vatican.va/content/francesco/en/homilies/2015/documents/papa-francesco_20150125_vespri-conversione-san-paolo.html.

Pope Francis has recounted how the evangelical Pentecostal pastors of Buenos Aires reached out to him.[13] After becoming pope, Francis preached to a Pentecostal community known as the Evangelical Church of Reconciliation in Caserta, Italy, led by Pastor Giovanni Traettino, whom the pope has called "a very dear friend."[14] In his address to that group, the pope preached that the Holy Spirit is the source of both diversity and unity in the Church: "He does both these things: he creates the diversity of charismata and then he makes harmony of the charismata." The pope also asked for their forgiveness, as the "Pastor of Catholics," for those Catholics who "denounced Pentecostal brothers for being 'exuberant.'"[15]

If one considers Pope Francis' insightful teachings on the Holy Spirit and his warm, positive relations with Pentecostals, it is no surprise that Pope Francis is in a good position

13. Francis, Address to Pentecostal Church of Reconciliation in Caserta, July 28, 2014, http://w2.vatican.va/content/francesco/en/speeches/2014/july/documents/papa-francesco_20140728_caserta-pastore-traettino.html. "We are on this path of unity, between brothers and sisters. Some may be shocked: 'But the Pope went to the Evangelicals!' He went to visit his brothers! Yes! Because—and what I speak is the truth—they first came to visit me in Buenos Aires. And there is a witness here: Jorge Himitian can tell the story of when they came, they made the approach. . . . And thus this friendship began, this closeness between the pastors of Buenos Aires, and here today. I thank you. I ask you to pray for me, I need it . . . that at least I won't be so bad. Thank you!"

14. Francis, Address to Members of the "Catholic Fraternity of Charismatic Covenant Communities and Fellowships," October 31, 2014, https://w2.vatican.va/content/francesco/en/speeches/2014/october/documents/papa-francesco_20141031_catholic-fraternity.html.

15. Francis, Address to Pentecostal Church of Reconciliation.

to understand and pastor Catholics in the Renewal. Yet even knowing that, I still find his awareness of what the Renewal stands for and his pastoral guidance to be a clear sign that his charism as our chief pastor on earth is present and potentially very fruitful—that is, if we hear and heed his words.

Pope Francis has addressed the Renewal in various ways. In his pontificate, he has met with representatives of International Catholic Charismatic Renewal Services (ICCRS) and leaders of the Catholic Fraternity of Charismatic Covenant Communities and Fellowships. He has strongly urged these two service organizations to work together, as they have been serving different groups within the Renewal and have sometimes been at odds. Both are recognized organizations of Pontifical Right, overseen by the recently formed Dicastery for Laity, Family, and Life. Pope Francis has thanked them for starting to work toward greater unity by locating their offices in Rome in the same building.[16]

Pope Francis has frequently warned the Renewal, especially its leaders, against excessive organization ("Yes, you need organization, but never lose the grace of letting God be God!"). The Holy Spirit must be given freedom to act. The pope even counsels leaders of prayer groups (he prefers the term "servants" over "leaders") not to control who can receive prayer

---

16. Pope Francis expressed his gratitude for this "witness to unity and grace"; see Francis, Address to Members of the "Catholic Fraternity of Charismatic Covenant Communities and Fellowships." He reiterated this in a message to the Catholic Fraternity on October 20, 2015, marking the silver jubilee of the establishment of that fraternity as a private association of Papal Right.

for baptism in the Spirit, thus inadvertently becoming "managers" of grace instead of dispensers of grace.[17]

He also argues for a limited term of office for all those in leadership roles in the Renewal, aware of the temptations of power, which lead to vanity and other abuses. No one in leadership is irreplaceable—the one exception being those who have the charism of founding a new religious congregation. But the Renewal has no human founder, and so "an important service of leaders, of lay leaders, is to make those who will fill their posts at the end of their service grow and mature spiritually and pastorally."[18] It must be clear, the pope concludes, that "the only irreplaceable one in the Church [and in the Renewal] is the Holy Spirit, and Jesus is the only Lord."[19]

Pope Francis' view of national and international organizations that have emerged in the Renewal—covenant communities, service committees, and so on—can be summarized in two points: (1) They must not restrict the freedom of the Lord, the freedom of the Holy Spirit, to act and to be the true leader of the Renewal and the source of all its graces. (2) All leadership roles in the Renewal exist only to serve the Lord, the Church, and the Renewal. They should rotate and never become the

---

17. Francis, Address to Participants in the 37th National Convocation of the Renewal in the Holy Spirit.

18. Francis, Address to the Renewal in the Holy Spirit Movement, July 3, 2015, http://w2.vatican.va/content/francesco/en/speeches/2015/july/documents/papa-francesco_20150703_movimento-rinnovamento-spirito.html.

19. Ibid.

means to exalt a person or lead to authoritarianism, vanity, or unjust financial gain.

"A Current of Grace": Pope Francis' Pastoral Vision for the Renewal

In reading Pope Francis' 2014 and 2015 addresses to the Catholic Fraternity, ICCRS, and convocations of the Italian Renewal of the Spirit, one discovers that Pope Francis has a clear and definite understanding of the purpose of the Catholic Charismatic Renewal in God's plan. He also has developed very clear directives for the Renewal based on this pastoral vision. What is the Renewal? Pope Francis describes it as a "current of grace" in the Church, and he makes it clear that he believes that it is intended by God to benefit the whole Church.

On July 3, 2015, in St. Peter's Square, Pope Francis declared, "[The] Charismatic Renewal is a Pentecostal grace for the whole Church. Agreed?" Later, in the same address, he said it is a "current of grace, which is for the Church and for the world."[20]

At the opening of this same address, he explained that this idea of the Renewal as a "flow" or "current" of grace came from Cardinal Leon-Joseph Suenens, who said this in the homily of the Mass he celebrated in St. Peter's Basilica on Pentecost Monday 1975,

The first error that must be avoided is including the Charismatic Renewal in the category of a Movement. It is not a

---

20. Ibid.

specific Movement; the Renewal is not a Movement in the common sociological sense; it does not have founders, it is not homogeneous and it includes a great variety of realities; it is a current of grace, a renewing breath of the Spirit for all members of the Church, laity, religious, priests and bishops. It is a challenge for us all. One does not form part of the Renewal, rather, the Renewal becomes a part of us provided that we accept the grace it offers us.[21]

Pope Francis agrees with Cardinal Suenens.[22] In a message to the Catholic Fraternity on October 30, 2015, Pope Francis said that the worldwide Charismatic Renewal represents a "single current of grace." He continued,

On Pentecost 2017, it will be 50 years since the irruption of this current of grace in the Catholic Church. I have invited you to celebrate this Golden Jubilee with the Bishop of Rome at St. Peter's Square. Let it not be the celebration of a "movement,"

---

21. Ibid.

22. It is notable that in his 1998 address to the World Congress of Ecclesial Movements before Pentecost, then Cardinal Joseph Ratzinger distinguished between "movement, current, and action." The first characteristic of a movement is that it has a founder, a "charismatic leader," and takes "shape in concrete communities inspired by the life of their founder." A "current," according to Cardinal Ratzinger, eventually does take on "concrete" historical forms, but its origin is not in any founder or institution. He used the emergence of liturgical renewal efforts in the early twentieth century or the new flourishing of Marian devotion beginning in the nineteenth century as examples of currents (even though they were often called "movements"). Ratzinger, "Ecclesial Movements in the Church," 47.

which you are not! Let it be the renewal of Pentecost for the Church and the world, together with all the Christians who have lived the experience of "being born anew" Jesus spoke about with Nicodemus (John 3:3-6). The Church and the world need, today more than ever, the Holy Spirit! They need more than ever the announcement of the *Kerygma* proclaimed by Peter on the morning of Pentecost.[23]

How is the Church to respond to the seemingly inexorable tsunami of secularism and unbelief, especially in the culturally Western world? How can the embers of evangelization among Catholics be fanned into a flame? Pope Francis understands that the only suitable and effective answer is an outpouring of the Holy Spirit, and he sees the Renewal as a rich "current" of this grace already flowing in the Church worldwide.

Pope Francis also sees this as an *ecumenical* current of grace. He frequently reminds the Renewal of its ecumenical origins and identity, stressing that it must continue to be an instrument of God for fostering the restoration of unity among Christians. In his address to the Italian Renewal, Pope Francis observed,

> There is another strong sign of the Spirit in [the] Charismatic Renewal: the search for unity of the Body of Christ. You, Charismatics, have a special grace to pray and work for Christian unity, so that the current of grace may pass through all

23. Francis, Message to the Catholic Fraternity. https://godsdelight.org/library/outreach/ccr_resources/2015-11%20Pope%20Francis%20Letter%20to%20the%20CFCCCF%20+%20footnotes.pdf.

Christian Churches. Christian unity is the work of the Holy Spirit and we must pray together—spiritual ecumenism, the ecumenism of prayer. "But, Father, can I pray with an Evangelical, with an Orthodox, with a Lutheran?"—"You must, you must! You have received the same Baptism." We have all received the same Baptism; we are all going on Jesus' path, we want Jesus. . . . We must do everything in order to journey together: spiritual ecumenism, the ecumenism of prayer, the ecumenism of work, but of charity at the same time; the ecumenism of reading the Bible together. . . .

This current of grace passes through all Christian Confessions, all of us who believe in Christ—unity first of all in prayer. The work for Christian unity begins with prayer. Pray together.[24]

Pope Francis also speaks of an "ecumenism of blood," reminding us that when Christians are persecuted, past and present, the persecutors don't care about one's Christian confession or denomination. We are Christians, and as Pope St. John Paul II reminded us, the blood shed by all Christian martyrs is a powerful testimony to our common faith. Pope Francis notes that Blessed Pope Paul VI said the same about the Ugandan martyrs

---

24. Francis, Address to the Renewal in the Holy Spirit Movement. Pope Francis also stressed this in his message to the Catholic Fraternity on October 30, 2015, that "Christians should be united, as the Lord asks (John 17: 21-23), to give witness together to the Father's merciful love, which does not make any preference among people, love which is made known to us in Jesus Christ, Lord and Savior! . . . Do not forget your background, the Charismatic Renewal was born ecumenical. Ecumenism of the encounter in fraternal prayer, in the service to your neighbor, and in the prayer of intercession through our common martyrs."

of the mid-twentieth century, where Catholics and Anglicans died together.[25]

Besides Pope Francis' pastoral vision of the Renewal bringing the grace of Pentecost to the whole Church and advancing the cause of Christian unity, the Pope also sees the Renewal as another way that God is acting to reach out to the poor and the marginalized. In August 2014, during a pastoral visitation to South Korea, the pope spent three hours at the Catholic charismatic community known as Kkottongnae. This community's apostolate is to serve the poorest of the poor, the homeless, and the handicapped.

In this visit, the pope was greeted by 30,000 people connected with the community, which is like a small town. He first visited the House of Hope (for the handicapped), where he stayed for an hour and blessed and embraced them all. Then he met with 440 religious men and women at the Training Institute of Love. Finally, the pope went to the House of the Spirit of Love, where he met with 153 leaders of the community's Apostolate of the Laity.[26] This community's outreach to

---

25. Francis, Address to Renewal in the Holy Spirit Movement. See Pope John Paul II's encyclical, *Ut Unum Sint* [On Commitment to Ecumenism], May 25, 1995, §83, 84, http://w2.vatican.va/content/john-paul-ii/en/encyclicals/documents/hf_jp-ii_enc_25051995_ut-unum-sint.html.

26. "Pope visits Kkottongnae Community in South Korea," *ICCRS Newsletter,* Vol. XXXX, No. 5 (October–December 2014), 3. I had the privilege of meeting a large contingent of this Spirit-filled charismatic community in 2001 in Rome at a colloquium on healing co-sponsored by ICCRS and the Pontifical Council for the Laity.

the poor and those on the periphery is one of the fruits that Pope Francis sees flowing from the Renewal.

Pope Francis seems fully aware of the international scope of the Renewal. In fact, he knows it well enough to offer some specific pastoral directives.

Pope Francis' Directives to the Renewal

Pope Francis clearly has a pastoral vision for the Renewal; he also appears to have a pastoral plan for the Renewal, which he has expressed in public addresses to participants in the Italian Renewal in the Spirit and to ICCRS and the Catholic Fraternity.

The most important component of this plan, the pope repeatedly states, is for members of the Renewal to *spread the grace of baptism in the Holy Spirit* so that everyone may encounter Jesus Christ personally.[27]

In his address to the Italian Renewal in the Spirit at Olympic Stadium in Rome on June 1, 2014, Pope Francis presented

---

27. The first work of the Holy Spirit is to enable a person to know Jesus, that he is Lord—not just of the universe, but of one's own life. Likewise, the Spirit reveals that God the Father is "Abba," our loving Father in heaven. This revelation, which is the first and most important fruit of being baptized in the Holy Spirit, is also the first step of conversion (or a deeper or renewed conversion) to the Lord. Yes, the Holy Spirit also bestows gifts (charisms), but the Renewal, and Pope Francis, understand that the importance of being baptized in the Holy Spirit is first and foremost an awakening by the Holy Spirit of the grace of sacramental baptism that makes a person a child of God through faith and thereby invites him or her into a living, personal relationship with God.

a number of points that state succinctly what he expects of the Renewal. The first two are the key directives:

> They asked me to tell you what the Pope expects of you.
>
> The first thing is conversion to the love of Jesus which changes our lives and makes each Christian a witness to God's love. The Church expects this witness of Christian life from us, and the Holy Spirit helps us to live the Gospel fully and consistently for our own growth in holiness.
>
> I expect you to share with everyone in the Church the grace of baptism in the Holy Spirit (a phrase we find in the Acts of the Apostles).[28]

After these two key points, the pope added a few more things he expects from the Renewal:

> I expect you to evangelize with the word of God, which proclaims that Jesus lives and that he loves all men and women.
>
> To give a witness of spiritual ecumenism to all our brothers and sisters of other Churches and Christian communities who believe in Jesus as Lord and Savior. To remain united in the love that the Lord Jesus asks us to have for all people, and in prayer to the Holy Spirit for the attainment of this unity which is necessary for evangelization in the name of Jesus. . . .
>
> Be close to the poor and to those in need, so as to touch in their flesh the wounded flesh of Jesus. Please, draw near to them!

---

28. Francis, Address to Participants in the 37th National Convocation of the Renewal in the Holy Spirit.

> Seek unity in the renewal, because unity comes from the Holy Spirit and is born of the unity of the Trinity. Who is the source of division? The devil! Division comes from the devil. Flee from all infighting, please! Let there be none of this among you![29]

Even though these could be seen as general admonitions, these words of Pope Francis reflect both his close familiarity with the Renewal and his belief that the Renewal can be a significant force or resource to meet the needs of the Church and the world today. For example, a year later he elaborated on these first two directives about conversion and baptism in the Holy Spirit:

> This is the most important service—the most important that can be given to everyone in the Church. To help the People of God in their personal encounter with Jesus Christ, who changes us into new men and women, in little groups, humble but effective, because it is the Spirit at work.[30]

Those involved in the Renewal are certainly grateful to Pope Francis for meeting with Renewal leaders and groups and offering his encouragement, guidance, and prayers.

For the golden jubilee of the Catholic Charismatic Renewal, Pope Francis enthusiastically invited Renewal participants to celebrate with him at the Vatican on Pentecost 2017. In a private audience on April 25, 2016, Pope Francis met with an

---

29. Ibid.

30. Francis, Address to Renewal in the Holy Spirit Movement.

executive committee to plan this event. Besides encouraging those planning to go forward with courage despite opposition and to be prepared for the "surprises of the Holy Spirit," Pope Francis expressed his desire that this event would not be a celebration only for Catholic charismatics but also for other Christians. He noted that 2017 was also the five hundredth anniversary of the beginnings of the Protestant Reformation, a division that God wishes to overcome.[31]

Influences on Pope Francis' Understanding of the Renewal

How has Pope Francis come to appreciate and understand the Renewal? Three sources stand out to me. The first, previously mentioned, is the personal contacts he had with both evangelical Pentecostal leaders and the Catholic Charismatic Renewal in Buenos Aires.

The second is the great respect that Pope Francis appears to have for one of the first great advocates of the Renewal, Cardinal Leon-Joseph Suenens. In his 2014 meeting with the Italian Renewal in the Spirit, Pope Francis referred to the Malines Documents, theological and pastoral "position papers" on the Renewal that Cardinal Suenens initiated and coauthored, calling them "a guide, a reliable path to keep you from going astray." He listed the first three Malines Documents by name. It might appear surprising that a pope in the second decade

31. "Pope Francis received the CCR Golden Jubilee executive committee in a private audience," ICCRS news release, April 25, 2016, http://www.iccrs.org/en/pope-francis-received-the-ccr-golden-jubilee-executive-committee-in-a-private-audience/.

of the twenty-first century should call attention to guidelines for the Renewal written forty years prior, but that is what he has done, indicating that they are still important sources to guide the Renewal.[32]

A year later, in his address to the Italian Renewal gathered at St. Peter's, Pope Francis began his talk with a brief history of the Renewal and gave special mention to the importance of Cardinal Suenens and his associate, Veronica O'Brien, who urged Suenens to go to the United States to observe the Renewal in its early stages, which he did. Pope Francis referred to "the second volume of [Suenens'] memoirs," which recounts this trip. Pope Francis apparently has studied, and values, both the Malines Documents and Cardinal Suenens' memoirs.[33]

The third influence on Pope Francis' understanding and appreciation of the Renewal is his close acquaintance with Fr. Raniero Cantalamessa, OFM Cap, whom he reappointed at the beginning of his pontificate as the Preacher of the Papal Household. Fr. Cantalamessa has held this post since 1980 under three popes. In his address to the members to the Catholic Fraternity on October 31, 2014, Pope Francis referred to him as "our beloved Fr. Raniero." Anyone who has followed the development of the Renewal knows what a wonderful ambassador Fr. Cantalamessa has been for the Renewal, in addition to being one of the most insightful modern teachers on the Person and work of the Holy Spirit. Fr. Cantalamessa's

---

32. Francis, Address to Participants in the 37th National Convention of the Renewal.

33. Francis, Address to Renewal in the Holy Spirit Movement.

association, if not identification, with the Renewal has such weight, not just because of the respect and recognition he has gained by virtue of his role as papal preacher, but even more because of his knowledge of the Fathers of the Church and his years of studying Scripture and Catholic spiritual and theological tradition.

Yet this scholarship has, since 1980, been used primarily to preach God's word. Most of his published writings are transcriptions or adaptations of homilies or talks. In my college courses on the Holy Spirit, I have found his book *Come, Creator Spirit*, a collection of homilies on the ancient Christian prayer to the Holy Spirit (Veni, Creator Spiritus), to be incredibly rich.[34] For the Renewal, his two volumes entitled *Sober Intoxication of the Spirit* present practical teaching on the meaning of baptism in the Spirit, the use of the charisms, and many other topics.[35] Even though I could (and would like to) present a whole chapter on Fr. Cantalamessa as a tribute to him in recognition of his influence both on the Renewal itself and on the recent popes and Catholic hierarchy on behalf of

34. Raniero Cantalamessa, OFM Cap, *Come, Creator Spirit: Meditations on the Veni Creator*, trans. Denis Barrett and Marlene Barrett (Collegeville, MN: Liturgical Press, 2003).

35. Raniero Cantalamessa, OFM Cap, *Sober Intoxication of the Spirit: Filled with the Fullness of God*, trans. Marsha Daigle-Williamson (Cincinnati, OH: Servant/Franciscan Media, 2005), and *Sober Intoxication of the Spirit, Part Two: Born Again of Water and the Spirit*, trans. Marsha Daigle-Williamson (Cincinnati, OH: Servant/Franciscan Media, 2012). The title of these books is taken from a phrase attributed to St. Ambrose, which Blessed Paul VI addressed in remarks to the Renewal after the Pentecost Mass he celebrated with them on May 19, 1975.

the Renewal, I will not do so here. I recommend his autobiography, *Serving the Word: My Life,* to anyone who would like to hear his story in his own words and his reflections on many topics.[36]

Fr. Cantalamessa on the Grace of Baptism in the Holy Spirit

An aspect of Fr. Cantalamessa's teaching that deserves mention in this history of the Renewal is his statements on the importance of baptism in the Spirit *as a grace for the whole Church,*[37] if only because of their possible—and I would say likely—influence on Pope Francis. Fr. Cantalamessa understands baptism in

---

36. Raniero Cantalamessa with Aldo Maria Valli, *Serving the Word: My Life,* trans. Marsha Daigle-Williamson (Cincinnati, OH: Servant/Franciscan Media, 2015).

37. Fr. Cantalamessa is not the first person in the Renewal to teach this. Fr. Kilian McDonnell, OSB, wrote in 1989: "No claim is made that the baptism in the Holy Spirit is captive to the charismatic renewal. On the contrary, the claim is that, because it is integral to initiation, it belongs to the life of the whole church." Kilian McDonnell, OSB, *Open the Windows,* xxiv. This view was restated a year later in *Fanning the Flame,* a book edited by Frs. Montague and McDonnell: ". . . this gift of the baptism in the Holy Spirit belongs to the Christian inheritance of all those sacramentally initiated into the church." Kilian McDonnell and George T. Montague, eds., *Fanning the Flame: What Does Baptism in the Holy Spirit Have to Do with Christian Initiation?* (Collegeville, MN: Liturgical press, 1991), 10, and confirmed by Bishop Sam Jacobs, who wrote in an introductory letter to *Fanning the Flame,* dated December 7, 1990: "It is clear from the present document and many other studies that this grace of Pentecost, known as Baptism in the Holy Spirit, does not belong to any particular movement, but to the whole Church." (7).

the Spirit as a grace for all Catholics *and* for all Christians, as it is an ecumenical grace that transcends confessional boundaries. Fr. Cantalamessa's first significant experience of the Renewal was at the historic ecumenical charismatic conference in 1977 in Kansas City. Hence, Pope Francis' understanding of the Renewal as a grace to bring Christians together has been echoed and reinforced by his papal preacher.

What Fr. Cantalamessa explains most cogently and clearly is *why* baptism in the Spirit, as understood and promoted in the Renewal, is important for the whole Church today. His most complete and detailed explanation of this topic was presented in his address to an international colloquium on baptism in the Spirit, which was edited and republished as a chapter in his book *Sober Intoxication of the Spirit.*[38] There he explains that it is possible for the graces of a sacrament to remain "unreleased" and that one of the most frequent reasons for this situation is a lack of full or expectant faith on the part of the recipient of the sacrament. In the early Church, those baptized were mainly adults, who were in a better position to receive the sacraments

---

38. Chapter 3 of the first volume of Cantalamessa's *Sober Intoxication of the Spirit*, "The Outpouring or Baptism in the Holy Spirit," is the adaptation of a talk he presented at the International Colloquium on Baptism in the Holy Spirit cosponsored by ICCRS and the Pontifical Council for the Laity in Rome on March 17–20, 2011. Zenit published a similar talk by Fr. Cantalamessa on May 9, 2014, that was presented to the Catholic Fraternity in Norfolk, Virginia. The talk was entitled "The Baptism in the Spirit: A Grace for the Whole Church." See "Father Cantalamessa Explains Why 'Baptism in the Spirit' Is a Gift for the Whole Church," ZENIT, May 9, 2014, https://zenit.org/articles/father-cantalamessa-explains-why-baptism-in-the-spirit-is-a-gift-for-the-whole-church/.

of initiation with this sort of expectant faith. But today, especially in secularized societies that suppress or attack faith, the situation is different. Fr. Cantalamessa explains,

> The environments in which many children now grow up do not help faith to blossom. The same must often be said of the family, and more so of the child's school and even more so of our society and culture. This does not mean that in our situation today normal Christian life cannot exist or that there is no holiness or no charisms that accompany holiness. Rather, it means that instead of being the norm, it has become more and more of an exception.
>
> In today's situation, rarely, or never, do baptized people reach the point of proclaiming "in the Holy Spirit" that "Jesus is Lord!" And because they have not reached that point, everything in their Christian lives remains unfocused and immature. Miracles no longer happen. What happened with the people of Nazareth is being repeated: Jesus was not able to do many miracles there because of their unbelief (see Matthew 13:58).
>
> The outpouring of the Spirit, then, is a response by God to the dysfunction in which Christian life now finds itself.[39]

Fr. Cantalamessa recognizes that there are other ways in which the grace and power of the sacraments of initiation can be "released," such as at the renewal of baptismal vows during the Easter vigil, in undertaking spiritual exercises, or

---

39. Cantalamessa, *Sober Intoxication of the Spirit*, 47.

in making religious vows, called "a second baptism."[40] But he goes on to explain,

> Although I said the outpouring of the Spirit is not the only time of renewal of baptismal grace, it holds a very special place because it is open to all of God's people, big and small, and not just to certain privileged people who do the Ignatian spiritual exercises or take religious vows.[41]

The bottom line is that God has chosen to pour out his Spirit in a new way in our time through people who have discovered that when they join in prayer (and prayer is the key) to ask God for this grace of being baptized anew in the Holy Spirit, God responds. The Holy Spirit comes in a new and powerful way into people's lives. Fr. Cantalamessa insists that we remember that this is an action of God; even though preparation and instruction are important, we should not make too many demands or impose undue requirements on people seeking this grace. In addition, the prayer itself for the Holy Spirit to come should be simple and direct.[42]

In spite of his erudition, Fr. Cantalamessa has a wonderfully simple way of explaining what baptism in the Spirit is about. In a devotional article, he notes,

---

40. Ibid., 49.

41. Ibid., 50.

42. Ibid., 55.

Something happens when we listen carefully to the story of Pentecost. It's like what happens in the Eucharist. At the moment of consecration, the Church retells what Jesus did on the last night of his life: he took bread, broke it, and gave it to his disciples. When this story is recounted by an ordained priest in the Sacrament of the Eucharist, it actually *brings about* what it describes. What happened on Jesus' last night on earth happens again: the bread becomes the Body of Christ. Likewise, when we listen to the story of Pentecost with open, trusting hearts, the coming of the Holy Spirit can happen again in our day. . . .

Do you want to discover more of the joy and power of this new world, this new dimension of life? You can! Ask the Father for the grace of a new Pentecost. You have Jesus' word that this best of Fathers will not fail to give the Holy Spirit to all who ask (Luke 11:13).[43]

43. Raniero Cantalamessa, OFM Cap, "The Love of God Poured Out: Pentecost Is Meant for All of Us," in *The Word Among Us*, Vol. 35, No. 5 (May 2016), 5, 15.

Fr. Cantalamessa calls this grace a "spiritual event"[44] and an "experience" in a person's life:

> Being filled with the Holy Spirit is more than a promise from Jesus; it's an experience. Imagine the life of the Trinity—divine life itself—filling a person's heart! Pentecost was the moment when each of the apostles had the overwhelming experience of being loved by God. . . .
>
> Do you think this was an unconscious event for the apostles—something that took place deep down in their hearts but that they didn't feel? Certainly not! This wasn't like a heart transplant with full anesthesia. No, they *experienced* something. From that moment on, they were new persons, full of courage, fearlessly preaching Jesus. Only love can achieve that.[45]

I think it is this understanding of baptism in the Holy Spirit that encouraged Pope Francis to charge those in the Renewal to bring this grace to the whole Church. Yes, the charisms

---

44. Cantalamessa, *Sober Intoxication of the Spirit*, 56, 57. "When we talk about the mode of this grace, we can speak of it as a new coming of the Holy Spirit, as a new sending of the Spirit by the Father through Jesus Christ or as a new anointing corresponding to a new level of grace. In this sense the outpouring, although not a sacrament, is nevertheless an event, a *spiritual event*. This definition corresponds most closely to the reality of the thing. It is an *event*, something that happens and that leaves a sign, creating something new in a life. It is a *spiritual* event, rather than an outwardly visible, historical one, because it happens in a person's spirit, in the interior part of a person, where others may not recognize what is happening. Finally, it is spiritual because it is the work of the Holy Spirit."

45. Cantalamessa, "The Love of God Poured Out," 6–7.

are also important. Fr. Cantalamessa has explained that the work of the Holy Spirit in the Church and in people's lives has both a *sanctifying* dimension, leading people to Jesus and to become his disciples, and a *charismatic* dimension, giving each person particular gifts to build up the Church and for her mission.[46] When people encounter the Lord in a new and deeper way through baptism in the Spirit, they are (generally, if properly instructed) open and ready to receive the charisms, and they desire to use them to minister to God (in worship) and to others.

In his fifth Lenten homily to the papal household in 2015, Fr. Cantalamessa provided a fitting summary of the impact of the Renewal in the Church today: "The primary goal of Christian life is once again shown to be, as St. Seraphim of Sarov said, 'the acquisition of the Holy Spirit.'" He then quotes St. John Paul II:

> The Catholic charismatic movement is one of the many fruits of the Second Vatican Council, which, like a new Pentecost, led to an extraordinary flourishing in the Church's life of groups and movements particularly sensitive to the action of the Spirit." . . . How many lay faithful—men, women, young people, adults, and the elderly—have been able to experience in their own lives the amazing power of the Spirit and his gifts! How many people have rediscovered the faith, the joy

---

46. Cantalamessa explained this in the complete version of his address to the International Colloquium on Baptism in the Holy Spirit in 2011. Participants received copies at the colloquium.

of prayer, the power and beauty of the Word of God, translating all this into generous service in the Church's mission! How many lives have been profoundly changed! (Address to Leaders of the Renewal in the Spirit, April 4, 1998)[47]

47. "Fr. Cantalamessa's 5th Lenten Homily 2015: East and West Before the Mystery of Salvation," ZENIT, March 27, 2015, https://zenit.org/articles/fr-cantalamessa-s-5th-lenten-homily-2015/.

Chapter 8

A Current of Grace
for the Whole Church

Where is the Renewal today? I have seen statistics estimating that between 120 to 150 million Catholics have been baptized in the Holy Spirit, which is 12 to 15 percent of Catholics worldwide.[1] Of course, many of these were baptized in the Spirit and were active in the Renewal at some point but are no longer associated with it. (Some call these "post-charismatics.") It is nearly impossible to estimate the number of active members, as this is a current of grace and not an organized movement with formal membership. I personally know many people who were baptized in the Spirit and belonged to prayer groups or covenant communities in years past but now would not identify themselves as "charismatic" or part of this Renewal in the Holy Spirit.

Yet most of the people I have known through the Renewal have remained committed Catholics who are active in their parishes or who have joined other Catholic groups or movements. God touched their lives through this current of grace and continues to guide and use them in advancing his kingdom, and this

---

1. In 2012, ICCRS estimated that 120 million Catholics have been baptized in the Holy Spirit in 238 countries. Dr. Mary Healy, "Document on the Baptism in the Spirit," *ICCRS Newsletter,* Vol. XXXVII, No. 5 (October–December 2011), http://www.iccrs.org/_files/files/Newsletter/2009to2012/NL11-5_En.pdf.

is a good fruit of this Renewal that should not be neglected in telling its story.

Even though the growth of the Renewal has slowed and even declined in some parts of the world, such as in North America, it is spreading and growing in other parts of the world, including Africa, Latin America, and parts of Asia. Each country has its own story about the birth, spread, and impact of the Renewal there.

However, many people wonder (and some have asked me these questions): Where is the Renewal going from here? Is it destined to decline and disappear? I have heard a Renewal leader say, probably off the record, that the Renewal in North America is a dying movement because of the declining number of prayer groups and the aging of the original participants, who are not being replaced by the young. Although I am not a prophet—and prophecy would be one good avenue to seek the answer to this question—I *am* a church historian who has a special interest in spiritual movements and renewal movements in the history of Christianity. Based on this vantage point and on my own experience and prayerful thought, I will close this book with some of my own observations and even predictions.

The key factor, next to God's grace, determining the future of the Renewal in the Catholic Church is how Catholics, and especially the pastors of the Catholic Church, respond to this current of grace (regardless of what it is labeled, whether Charismatic Renewal, or Renewal in the Spirit or, as the French call it, the "effusion" or outpouring of the Spirit). God does not force his freely given grace and gifts upon anyone, and that includes every Catholic, every Christian, and every church leader. The Renewal might not achieve the full effects God desires—or may even die prematurely—if the grace being offered is met with indifference, skepticism, or rejection. As Pope Paul VI said, this Renewal is a chance or an opportunity for the Church, and so what happens to the Renewal depends not just on God but also on the human response to this grace. For example, if Catholics don't accept or don't find a way to use the charisms of prophecy or speaking in tongues or healing when God is offering these gifts, the gifts, rejected, will die out—except, possibly, in pockets within the Church where people remain open to receiving them in faith.

Let's consider the charisms—one important aspect of this Renewal. The Second Vatican Council opened the Catholic Church to some authentic and necessary forms of renewal. A renewal is not something totally new, but a rediscovery and reawakening of things that are part of the fullness of the Church, a part of her nature, so to speak.[2] We can look back in history to discover aspects of the Church that previously were part of her life or mission but became neglected or forgotten over time.

One example of this is the Church's worship. Vatican II opened the Church to the renewal of the liturgy, including the sacraments, that reawakened or restored elements that were present in the early Church but became neglected or obscured

---

2. Catholics, by the way, believe that by God's mercy our Church faithfully preserves the fullness of Christianity and that Catholicism is full Christianity, not Christianity with some foreign or extraneous elements "added on."

over time. Another example is biblical renewal, which brought Catholics back to reading the word of God in Sacred Scripture and to a fuller and more vibrant proclamation of that word by the ordained ministers. Extensive efforts were made after the council, by both clergy and laity, to bring about these renewals and to make them accepted and effective in the Church's life. We also have had concerted efforts to promote the renewal of religious life, the priesthood and priestly formation, and the more active role of laypeople in the Church. All of these have required significant and concerted effort to bring about what the council called for. Even though these renewals are not yet finished or perfectly accomplished, great strides have been made in the past fifty years to create a climate in which these renewed aspects of the Church's life are recognized and supported by all Catholics.

The Second Vatican Council also called for a renewal or reawakening of the charisms in the life of the Church. We have already discussed the council's teaching that these charisms be gratefully welcomed and used in the Church. And, lo and behold, two years after the council ended, Catholics began to receive the full range of charisms that we read about in the New Testament. These charisms were not understood by the council to be for a particular group or movement but for the whole Church—a part of our ancient Christian heritage that had been neglected and even forgotten by many. The so-called "charismatic" renewal was, in the council's teaching, part of the renewal that was to affect and transform the life of the whole Church—a renewal of the charismatic dimension of the

Church's life (like the renewal of the liturgy, sacraments, Scripture, the laity, religious life, catechetics, and so forth).

The question is, has this been done? If we are asking about the future of the charismatic dimension of the current of grace called the Renewal, the question is whether the hierarchy and members of the Catholic Church are ready to have the whole Church rediscover her charismatic dimension and to discuss how *all* the charisms that God is lavishing upon us can become part of the normal life of the Catholic Church, even in the parish. I am not saying that this is easy. It is still difficult, for example, for many Catholics to think that reading and studying the Bible regularly is really a Catholic practice and not something Protestant. It is difficult for many lay Catholics to think it is part of their Catholic calling to be active in the Church (besides going to Sunday Mass) or to talk about their faith with others in view of leading them to Christ and his Church. But in my opinion, after fifty years since the council's close and the beginning of the Renewal, there are still many pastors and even committed Catholics who think that charisms are either just a fancy term for natural talents or that they are some superspiritual things possessed by that strange, cultish group—"the charismatics." This, I believe, is the greatest failure in the teaching and implementation of all the "renewals" called for by Vatican II.

However, on a more hopeful note, there is a way that the charismatic dimension of the Church can be rediscovered and fostered in the way God desires that is less painful than trying to tell Catholics about spiritual gifts or charisms when they have no basis for understanding this from their own experience or their knowledge of the Catholic Church. A better way is the way that God has acted in the Renewal: people are awakened in their faith and personal knowledge of God through being baptized in the Holy Spirit, and then, in addition, the Spirit lavishes the charisms upon them "to each one individually as he wills" (1 Corinthians 12:11). We see this at Pentecost and in many subsequent accounts of conversion in the Acts of the Apostles: people receive the Holy Spirit (are "baptized in the Spirit") and *then* they speak in tongues, prophesy, hunger for God's word, and so on. This seems to be *God's* way of awakening or reawakening the charisms.

When people are seeking the Lord and are open to whatever he wants to do in their lives, if they are then baptized in the Holy Spirit, they normally receive the charisms with gratitude. (If they consciously refuse a charism, of course, God doesn't force it upon them.) At this point, they are ready to receive instruction and guidance as to the proper use, within the community of the Church, of the charism(s) they have received. The next step is to find people who are able to instruct them about the charisms and, more important, to locate places and ways in which those who have received these spiritual gifts can use them openly and fruitfully in the life of the Church. But the first step is for the full range of biblical charisms to be recognized, accepted, and welcomed by Catholics.

So far, however, the only place in the Catholic Church in which charisms such as prophecy, words of knowledge, speaking in tongues, exhortation, and (with some exceptions) healing are "accepted with gratitude" (*CCC*, 800; cf. *Apostolicam Actuositatem*, 3) are in charismatic prayer groups and covenant communities.

What will happen to this current of grace? It seems to me that there are, broadly speaking, two possible directions or scenarios for the future of the Renewal in the Catholic Church. The first one, in my opinion, is more likely because it is the way the Renewal is currently being viewed and "managed" in the Catholic Church. Unless there are some fairly significant changes in the Church's pastoral approach to the Renewal, inertia will win out. Let's look at this first scenario.

Scenario One: The Current Trajectory of the Renewal

This scenario presupposes that God will continue to offer the powerful grace of the Holy Spirit to renew the faith and lives of people who seek to be baptized in the Holy Spirit and that God will continue to bless these people with the full range of charisms, including those listed by Sts. Peter and Paul in their epistles. If God does not do this, "all bets are off," and the Renewal will immediately die because it is essentially a gift of God to his people—a "current of grace," as Pope Francis calls it.

The present pastoral approach of the Catholic Church's leadership, however, is (in most places) *not* to recognize and promote the Renewal as a current of grace for the renewal of the whole Church (in contrast to the way Catholic leadership has recognized and promoted the biblical movement, the liturgical movement, the call for an active apostolate of the laity, and so forth). Instead, Catholic leadership has tended to view the Renewal as a particular movement in the Church (even though Pope Francis insists that it is not), instead of as a current of grace for the renewal of the whole Church. If it is treated as movement, the Renewal will continue, as all movements eventually do, to take on some distinctive institutional forms. An example of a movement that soon took the form of a religious order would be Franciscanism. The institutional forms of the Renewal are generally prayer groups/meetings and covenant communities, although there are also "houses of prayer," retreat centers, service committees, and liaisons that foster, support, and serve the Renewal.

Over the course of time, some movements die out when their membership declines or their institutional forms fail or no longer have a compelling purpose (which itself leads to membership decline). In the Renewal in the West, many prayer groups have disappeared because they don't have a stable institutional form. When leadership changes or leaves, or when the membership declines beyond a viable point, the group disbands. Sometimes parish prayer groups are active because of the involvement or support of the parish priest or pastoral associate, but when this changes, the group shrinks or disbands. Covenant communities tend to be more stable because they have more clearly defined institutional elements and usually a more stable leadership structure, but unless they attract new members, especially younger members, they too are subject to decline.

Another indicator of the future of the Renewal in this scenario is whether new prayer groups and covenant communities are being established: is the movement growing? The emergence—or lack thereof—of new prayer groups and/or charismatic communities is a measure of growth or decline. In some parts of the world, such as Africa and Latin America, the Renewal is in fact growing, whereas in Europe and North America, there appears to be more of a holding pattern or decline.

Behind all of this is a certain understanding of the Renewal that prevails throughout the Catholic Church: that the Renewal is not a current of grace for the whole Church. In this view, baptism in the Spirit and reception of most of the charisms described in the New Testament do not make you a fuller, better, "normal" Catholic but distinguishes you as a charismatic who should "keep your spiritual experiences and your charisms in your prayer meeting or charismatic community" but *not* in normal Catholic or parish life.

Of course, it is this prevailing attitude that makes Catholics involved in the Renewal feel marginalized and has even caused some to leave the Catholic Church, despairing that the Church can never be a place where the power of the Spirit and the charisms are really welcomed. Yes, Pope Francis exhorts the Renewal to share baptism in the Spirit with the whole Church, but what if this seems to be a message that few Catholics (and fewer pastors and priests) are really open to hearing? Jesus told a parable about sowing seeds (Matthew 13:1-23), and certainly Catholics in the Renewal must heed the Holy Father and continue to witness to the love and power of God that they have experienced in the Renewal, even when the seed of their testimony falls on rocky ground or among thorns. Like St. Peter, we can't help but testify to "what we have seen and heard" (Acts 4:20). But for many in the Renewal, this task of re-evangelization is not an easy one and requires faith and perseverance.

Yes, we have heard the prudent advice about being patient and not being pushy about the Renewal, especially with your pastor. I agree that charismatics must be there to serve in the ordinary ministries and tasks of parish life if they are to gain a hearing. I know many people in the Renewal who have been doing this for years. But at what point can one say, "Father, we really need a Life in the Spirit Seminar in our parish, and we are ready to do it, with your blessing"? And at what point is it right to ask, "Father, we have people with charisms of prophecy and healing and words from the Lord to build up our parish community in faith. How can we use them, and not just in our prayer meeting?"

In scenario one, it is possible that the Renewal will begin to influence the mainstream Catholic Church, for nothing is impossible for God. But what is lacking is an understanding that the Renewal is a current of grace for the *whole* Church. Unless something changes, the Renewal will be like other movements that continue to exist only in some para-ecclesial institutional forms, such as prayer meetings and covenant communities. As long as God continues to baptize in the Spirit, to renew Christian initiation, and to give the full range of charisms, these groups may continue to serve those who are seeking or who desire to live a fuller Christian life in the Spirit.

I agree with Pope Francis that the Renewal must always remember that its greatest gift of the Spirit to the Church is worship and praise. In a meeting with the Catholic Fraternity, he said,

> The Charismatic Renewal has reminded the Church of the necessity and importance of the prayer of praise. When we speak of the prayer of praise in the Church, Charismatics come to mind. When I spoke of the prayer of praise during a homily at Mass in Santa Marta, I said it is not only the prayer of Charismatics but of the entire Church! It is the recognition of the Lordship of God over us and over all creation expressed through dance, music and song.

> I would like to revisit with you a few passages from that homily: "The prayer of praise is a Christian prayer, for all of us. In the Mass every day, when we sing the 'Holy, Holy, Holy,' this is a prayer of praise: we praise God for his greatness because he is great. And we address him with beautiful words because it pleases us to do this. The prayer of praise bears fruit in us." . . .

> Together with the prayer of praise, the prayer of intercession is, in these days, a cry to the Father for our Christian brothers and sisters who are persecuted and murdered, and for the cause of peace in our turbulent world. Praise the Lord at all times, never cease to do so, praise him more and more, unceasingly.[3]

---

3. Francis, Address to Members of the "Catholic Fraternity of Charismatic Covenant Communities and Fellowships." He refers to a homily he gave at Casa St. Marta on January 28, 2014, http://w2.vatican.va/content/francesco/en/cotidie/2014/documents/papa-francesco-cotidie_20140128_prayer-praise.html.

It is also true that even in this scenario in which the Renewal does not affect mainstream Catholic life, there will still be ministries and outreaches of the Renewal that will reach countless souls and advance the mission of the Catholic Church. Merely the existence of faith-filled Catholics who belong to prayer groups and covenant communities is a witness to others and to the Church that Christianity is not just a once-a-week commitment. There are many "intentional disciples" of Jesus in these prayer groups and communities in the Renewal that the Church and the world need.

There are also many outreaches for evangelization, service to the poor, pro-life activities, healing ministries, and other outreaches that were founded by people who have been touched and motivated by the Holy Spirit through the Renewal. I think of Renewal Ministries, Family Missions Company, Jim Cavnar's Cross Catholic Outreach, LAMP Catholic Ministries, the International Programme of Catholic Evangelization (now called Institute for World Evangelisation: ICPE Mission), and Caritas in Veritate, just to name a few. Franciscan University of Steubenville would have been a casualty of the economic and enrollment crisis of the early 1970s if it had not been for its Spirit-filled president, Fr. Michael Scanlan, TOR.[4] In Brazil a Jesuit priest active in the Renewal, Fr. Edward Dougherty, founded Brazil's Seculo 21 Catholic satellite television channel, and Mother Angelica was involved in the Renewal in the early days of EWTN (while Johnnette Benkovic and Ralph

_____

4. Michael Scanlan, TOR, with James Manney, *Let the Fire Fall*, 3ʳᵈ Edition (Steubenville, OH: Franciscan University of Steubenville, 2016).

Martin continue this charismatic heritage on this network and in their respective ministries).

Though it is difficult to quantify, the Renewal has strengthened priestly and religious life and has contributed to many vocations, as then Cardinal Ratzinger observed in *The Ratzinger Report*. In the United States, Franciscan University of Steubenville began Renewal-oriented summer conferences for priests, deacons, seminarians, and religious in the mid-1970s, which, except for the conference for women religious, continue to this day. The Fraternity of Priests is a support system for priests that emerged from the Renewal, and a few religious communities identify themselves as charismatic, such as The Companions of the Cross in Canada and the Brothers of the Beloved Disciple in San Antonio, Texas.

Publications and media ministries that originated in the Renewal continue to flourish. Besides television, Bible study/liturgical magazines such as *The Word Among Us* and, previously, *God's Word Today* have been exemplary resources. Fr. Dave Pivonka, TOR, has begun a powerful ministry promoting the work of the Holy Spirit. (See his website, www.thewildgooseisloose.com, and his recent book, *The Breath of God*.[5]) Servant Books, now an imprint of Franciscan Media, was established to publish books of special interest to those in the Renewal. The Word Among Us Press, Paraclete Press, and others have done the same.

---

5. Dave Pivonka, TOR, *The Breath of God: Living a Life Led by the Holy Spirit* (Notre Dame, IN: Ave Maria Press, 2015).

We should also mention evangelistic youth outreaches that have roots in or connections to the Renewal. The Steubenville Youth Conferences (for high school-aged youth) have reached tens of thousands of people since the mid-1970s. NET Ministries, founded by Mark Berchem, has traveling ministries reaching out to this age group as well. Franciscan University of Steubenville graduate Curtis Martin is founder and president of Fellowship of Catholic University Students (FOCUS), forming Catholic disciples on college campuses. The ministries University Christian Outreach (UCO) and St. Paul's Outreach are charismatic outreaches to college and university students in the United States.

ChristLife, founded by Dave Nodar, is a program that brings baptism in the Spirit into parishes, and the Renewal Ministries DVD presentation *As By a New Pentecost* is an effective adaptation of the Life in the Spirit Seminars for parishes, prayer groups, or charismatic communities, with talks given by pioneers in the Renewal, including Patti Gallagher Mansfield, Dave Mangan, Ralph Martin, Sr. Ann Shields, and Peter Herbeck. These are just some of the fruits of the Renewal today, and these are mainly just in the United States.

So even if the Renewal does not come to be seen and accepted as a current of grace for all in the Church, those who have been touched by this grace and continue to respond to it will likely continue to make valuable contributions to the Church's life and mission.

Scenario 2: The Renewal as a Current of Grace for the Whole Church

In the first scenario, we see what has happened and what is likely to happen in the future as long as the Renewal continues to be dealt with pastorally as a movement in the Church that has taken on certain "institutional" form in prayer groups and covenant communities, as well as in certain ministries and outreaches that have emerged out of the Renewal at various points. There are also certain institutionalized alliances and service committees that provide some direction and leadership and that represent the Renewal in some way.

However, let's imagine a scenario in which the Renewal is truly understood and pastored as a current of grace for the whole Church. What would be different?

Let's say we are dealing with a situation in the Church in which people need to discover what it is to have a "living relationship" in prayer with the Father, Son, and Holy Spirit (CCC, 2565) or need to discover a "newness of life" in their Catholic faith (CCC, 1697; see Romans 6:4). Could it not become a normal practice to invite such people to pray for a fresh new sending of the Holy Spirit, who "renews us interiorly through a spiritual transformation" (CCC, 1695)? It could be explained to them that members of the parish or community will pray with them for a release or renewal of the grace of their baptism and confirmation. It would also be an opportunity for them to hear the basic message of the gospel, renounce sin, and renew their commitment to Christ. This is essentially what the Life in the Spirit Seminars and prayer to be baptized in the Holy Spirit are all about. Whatever it is called or however it is packaged, if people approach this with expectancy, as the presentations and the personal and group interactions help them to do, God will certainly bless them and act in their lives, as those in the Renewal can affirm.

This could also be approached and explained as a way of preparing to participate more fully in the Church's effort of evangelization. Many Catholics might like to be more effective ambassadors of their faith, but they understandably have fears and reservations. Why not invite them to consider Jesus' followers before and after Pentecost? If the coming of the Holy Spirit enabled the first, often fearful, followers of Christ to become witnesses who literally converted the world, why not ask the Holy Spirit to help us to be better witnesses to our faith? This could be presented in terms of a renewal or release of the grace of the Sacrament of Confirmation.

Again, I don't think it is necessary to use the terminology of baptism in the Holy Spirit or the format of a Life in the Spirit Seminar. One could speak of the fruits of a deeper prayer life, a greater interest in learning about the Bible and the Catholic faith, a new power to resist temptation and overcome habitual sins, a new joy in being a Catholic—all this and more that people in the Renewal have consistently reported as a result of praying for a greater outpouring or release of God's grace and the Holy Spirit. This is how the Renewal could be presented as a current of grace for the whole Church.

And what about charisms? The Second Vatican Council explained that charisms are a necessary part of the life of the whole Church. Pope St. John Paul II emphasized that the charisms are "co-essential" with the sacraments and the offices of the hierarchy; this is the very nature of the Church. The *Catechism of the Catholic Church* makes it absolutely clear that charisms are for everybody (799–801, especially paragraph 800). Still, the past fifty years have demonstrated that unless the pastors of the Catholic Church are proactive in promoting the aspects of renewal called for by the Second Vatican Council, they won't happen. As a church historian, I believe it is historically demonstrable that a council is only as good as its implementation. What is on paper in a church document or a catechism means little unless the pastors of the Church and the whole people of God take specific steps to ensure that the teaching is accepted and put into practice.

God has done his part. God has poured out the Holy Spirit and a rich abundance of charisms of all kinds on millions of Catholics. The task of the pastors and people of the Church is to accept them and make room for them, as long as they are authentic (*CCC*, 801).

There are many areas in which room can be made for the charisms. Take, for example, the use of charisms in the liturgy. One example, based on twenty-five years as a Catholic parish, was The Servants of Christ the King Fellowship Parish in Steubenville, Ohio, created by a bishop for members of a covenant community and anyone else interested who wanted to join it. In our Sunday liturgy, we entered into a time of praise in the Spirit, praying or singing in tongues, after the Gloria. A few moments of unscripted, Spirit-led reverent praise and thanksgiving was offered at the elevation of the Sacred Body and Precious Blood of Jesus and again after the Great Amen. After Communion, often preceded by a time of meditative silence, sometimes the Spirit would inspire the congregation to sing in tongues, and/or sometimes one or two prophecies or an exhortation would be given before the Mass concluded with a final blessing.[6]

The worship music, of course, was something that the whole congregation entered into wholeheartedly and joyfully. The Mass was a little longer than the average parish Mass, usually about seventy-five minutes, followed by informal fellowship after Mass outside the church. It was a liturgy that allowed the grace of the Renewal and the charisms to be expressed as an integral part of the life of the Catholic Church and not as some separate meeting or activity. Some liturgies, such as our Easter Vigil Mass, were so rich and joyful that my family will never forget them. The parish continued under three bishops until it was consolidated with four other parishes due to the declining number of Catholics in Steubenville. A similar type of liturgy was common on Sundays at Franciscan University of

6. There are those who say all this is inappropriate in the liturgy. Could it not be that allowing a few minutes of Spirit-led praise and thanksgiving and an openness to hearing a word from the Lord is one way of fulfilling what the Second Vatican Council's *Sacrosantum Consilium* [Constitution on the Sacred Liturgy] called the main purpose of its liturgical renewal, that is, to promote "the full, conscious and active participation" of all the faithful (14)? In any case, three consecutive bishops of the diocese approved this, and I see no reason why other bishops elsewhere could not do the same.

Steubenville for at least two decades, the late seventies through the mid-nineties. There are Catholic parishes, such as Christ the King in Ann Arbor, Michigan, that have vibrant liturgies incorporating the charisms at Mass and other services to this day.

Today, in particular areas where there are a large number of Catholics in the Renewal, this might be a good way for the bishop and the clergy to demonstrate that the Renewal is truly at the heart of the Church. Pope Francis often notes that unity does not mean uniformity. Every liturgy, even when the rubrics are carefully observed, does not need to be exactly the same, as the existence of different rites in the Catholic Church demonstrates.

What if there are not enough Catholics in the Renewal in a particular diocese to justify a parish having weekly worship in which the "charisms of the word" are welcomed and expressed? In some places, the bishop has authorized Masses in which charisms are exercised. Sometimes prayer for healing is incorporated, which recognizes that, following the example of Jesus and the apostles, the charism of healing is a gift that is always needed in the Church.

I would like to propose that if there is resistance to the use of the charisms in the liturgy in some dioceses, the faithful be granted the right to request it and receive it. If Catholics can request and receive permission to celebrate the Tridentine Mass as an Extraordinary Form of the liturgy, why should Catholics who desire to exercise the charisms and to praise God vocally in appropriate places in the liturgy not be offered the same privilege, especially if "charisms are to be accepted with gratitude by the person who receives them and by all members of the Church as well" (CCC, 800)?

The point is that this second scenario, in which the Renewal is truly seen as a current of grace for the whole Church, will only happen if the pastors of the Catholic Church are in agreement and are proactively supportive and promoting ways in which the grace of this Renewal can flow into the life of the Church. This has happened with the liturgical renewal, the biblical renewal, the renewal of the laity and the family, and even, in some ways, the pro-life movement, which rightfully is recognized as a hallmark of the Catholic Church today.

The baptism in the Holy Spirit is not a threat to the Church. It is a grace to lead Catholics, and all people, into a deep, personal encounter with the living God, unleashing power for service, evangelization, prayer, passion for reading God's word in Scripture, and many other good things. The charisms are not reserved only for meetings of a certain group in the Church; they are God's tools, God's resource, for building up the body of Christ in service, prayer, and ministry.

For this to happen, a change in mentality needs to take place. The eleventh commandment of Catholicism, "Don't rock the boat," has to go out the window, which means making room for the Holy Spirit to transform and empower the Church in ways we cannot, even with the best planning and effort. I think Pope Francis knows this, but the pope can't accomplish it by himself. He needs the whole Church, and especially her pastors, to be open to the grace that God is offering to his body, the Church.

Yet for this second scenario to unfold, people involved in the Renewal also need to change. Pope Francis has given the Renewal some clear directives. We have to be more radically open to the Holy Spirit and to reach out to the poor and those on the periphery. (He has said that these people need baptism in the Holy Spirit as well, not just material assistance.) We have to be more ecumenical. Pope Francis has challenged the Catholic Renewal to lead the way in ecumenical relations, even those communities and organizations that consider themselves exclusively Catholic. We have to seek unity within the Renewal, putting aside jealousy, gossip, and infighting for recognition or position, and collaborate in ways we have not done previously. All in the Renewal must guard against pride and elitism and seek to work in close communion with our pastors and fellow Catholics. Pope Francis himself summarized some of his exhortations to the Renewal in an address to the Catholic Fraternity in Rome on October 31, 2014:

Remember: seek the unity which is the work of the Holy Spirit and do not be afraid of diversity. The breathing of Christians draws in the new air of the Holy Spirit and then exhales it upon the world: it is the prayer of praise and missionary outreach. Share baptism in the Holy Spirit with everyone in the Church. Spiritual ecumenism and the ecumenism of blood. The unity of the Body of Christ. Pre pare the Bride for the Bridegroom who comes! One Bride only! (Revelation 22:17).[7]

It has often been said that the goal of the Renewal is to disappear into the life of the Church. The goal of the Renewal is a Church renewed and living by the power of the Holy Spirit. This is the hope expressed in this second scenario. It will happen if the Church finds ways to incorporate into parish life prayer for the Holy Spirit to come to renew the graces of baptism, confirmation, and Pentecost, which will empower her members to share their faith more freely and openly with others, to serve the needy, and to seek God's kingdom first. When Catholics can confidently say that Jesus is the Lord of their lives and pray in an intimate relationship with the Father, Son, and Holy Spirit, the grace of the Renewal will have accomplished its purpose. And when using the charisms is as normal and integral a part of Catholic life as praying the Rosary or going to Mass and receiving Holy Communion, and no one is singled out as being charismatic any more than having a devotion to Mary or the saints, then the Renewal will be flowing as a current of grace along with many others in the Church.

There still may be charismatic groups that meet for fellowship, prayer, mutual support, and service. But they will be just as normal as Catholics going to Eucharistic adoration or serving at the local soup kitchen. The charisms and this Renewal will have found their place in the rich tapestry of Catholic life.

Come, Holy Spirit!

7. Francis, Address to Members of the "Catholic Fraternity of Charismatic Covenant Communities and Fellowships."

Various Ways of Understanding Baptism in the Holy Spirit in a Catholic Theological Context

Besides Fr. Kilian McDonnell, OSB, an expert on Pentecostalism, and some early leaders of the Renewal who were theologians, such as Ralph Kiefer, Kevin Ranaghan, and Fr. Edward D. O'Connor, CSC, there were a number of other Catholic theologians and biblical scholars who published significant scholarly works on baptism in the Holy Spirit and related topics in the early 1970s, within three or four years of the Duquesne weekend. These works reflect the rapidity of the growth and the impact of this movement in the Catholic Church. Fr. Donald J. Gelpi, SJ, in his systematic study of Pentecostalism both historically and theologically, concluded that Pentecostalism is not inherently (necessarily) divisive and that prayer for baptism in the Spirit, though not a sacrament, can be very beneficial in opening a person to God and helping the person grow in docility to the action of the Holy Spirit.[1]

---

1. Donald J. Gelpi, SJ, *Pentecostalism: A Theological Viewpoint* (New York: Paulist Press, 1971), 181.

Appendix

Baptism in the Spirit as a Release of Sacramental Grace

In 1972, a theological treatise by English Dominican Simon Tugwell presented baptism in the Spirit as a manifestation of sacramental baptism—of the Holy Spirit dwelling within us—as well as a manifestation of real *metanoia* (conversion) that is essential to enter the kingdom of God. It is a gift of God that makes a person aware of the reality and power of the Holy Spirit dwelling within, inviting and empowering a person to live a truly changed life in which Jesus is truly Lord. Tugwell warned that there is the possibility of deception, of experiences that do not exalt Christ or result in true *metanoia,* and concluded,

> There must be no looking for "experiences," only a desire to see the work of Christ made real in us and through us. This must, of course, include experience; if our lives are truly being changed, they will feel different, and the range of our experiences will shift. But what we are seeking is God's will in Christ.[2]

The accounts of the early stages of Catholic Pentecostalism indicate that most of those attracted to this movement were not seeking a religious experience but were desiring to know God and to open their lives more fully to him and his will. Baptism in the Holy Spirit appeared as an opportunity,

2. Simon Tugwell, *Did You Receive the Spirit?* (Mahwah, NJ: Paulist Press, 1972), 48, 49.

a divine invitation, to open their lives to God in Jesus Christ and to all the gifts and graces that he desired to give them through the Holy Spirit.

By 1974, Catholic theological reflection on the charismatic movement and baptism in the Spirit had become even more widespread and significant. French theologian René Laurentin, in an important book that was translated and published in English in 1977, observed the emergence of two distinct schools of thought as to how baptism in the Spirit is to be understood in a Catholic framework. The first, and most prevalent among Catholic theologians, is to stress the relationship between Spirit-baptism and the sacraments of initiation, especially baptism and confirmation.

In fact, from the earliest days of the Renewal in the Catholic Church, the connection between Pentecostal "baptism in the Holy Spirit" and water baptism and/or the sacraments of initiation has been underscored by Catholic theologians of the Renewal. A document prepared by an international group of eight theologians invited by Cardinal Suenens to Malines, Belgium, in May 1974 was the first of a series that laid the theological foundation and justification for the Catholic Charismatic Renewal. The list of theological consultants for the Malines Document is impressive: Yves Congar, OP (France); Avery Dulles, SJ (United States); Michael Hurly, SJ (Ireland); Walter Kasper (Germany); René Laurentin (France); and Joseph

Ratzinger (Germany).[3] The Malines Document, as it came to be called, noted,

> Within the Catholic renewal the phrase "baptism in the Holy Spirit" refers to two senses or moments. First, there is the theological sense. In this sense, every member of the Church has been baptized in the Spirit because each has received sacramental initiation. Second, there is the experiential sense. It refers to the moment or the growth process in virtue of which the Spirit, given during the celebration of initiation, comes to conscious experience. When those within the Catholic renewal speak of "the baptism in the Holy Spirit," they are ordinarily referring to this conscious experience, which is the experiential sense.
>
> [Thus] when Roman Catholics use the phrase it usually means the breaking forth into conscious experience of the Spirit who was given during the celebration of initiation. In the Catholic renewal "baptism in the Holy Spirit" has these pronounced baptismal and sacramental accents which are not prominent in most other charismatic renewal movements.[4]

---

3. In addition to Catholic theologians, a number of prominent Catholic biblical scholars became involved in the Renewal in its early days and have written extensively on the charismatic movement, baptism in the Spirit, and the Holy Spirit from their expertise. These scholars include Fr. George Montague, SM, Fr. Francis Martin, Dr. Josephine Massingberde Ford, and Fr. William Kurz, SJ.

4. Malines Document I, 30–31.

One of the most comprehensive expositions of baptism in the Holy Spirit as an actualization or release of the Holy Spirit, who is conferred in the sacraments of initiation, is a 1991 study by Frs. Kilian McDonnell, OSB, and George T. Montague, SM, entitled *Christian Initiation and Baptism in the Holy Spirit: Evidence from the First Eight Centuries,* which draws upon both the New Testament and the Fathers of the Church.[5] Their conclusion is that when adults were baptized in the early Church, that which we call today "baptism in the Holy Spirit," with the charisms enumerated by St. Paul in 1 Corinthians, Romans, and Ephesians, was the normal and expected result of Christian initiation.

The same conclusion was reached by a group of American scholars who met in Techny, Illinois, in May 1990 and produced a short statement, edited by McDonnell and Montague, entitled *Fanning the Flame: What Does Baptism in the Holy Spirit Have to Do with Christian Initiation?*

> We, the undersigned, are writing to the bishops and pastoral leaders of the Catholic Church in the United States to share our conviction that what some early Christian authors called the "baptism in the Holy Spirit" is a key to living the Christian life to the fullest. In this document the "baptism in the Holy Spirit" refers to Christian initiation and to its reawakening in Christian experience. The early church used the baptism

---

5. Kilian McDonnell and George T. Montague, *Christian Initiation and Baptism in the Holy Spirit: Evidence from the First Eight Centuries* (Collegeville, MN: Liturgical Press, 1991; second revised edition, 1994).

in the Holy Spirit for Christian initiation. Using this phrase today for the later awakening of the original sacramental grace by no means signifies a second baptism. While not suggesting that the "baptism in the Holy Spirit" happens only in the charismatic renewal, our pastoral experience and theological reflection lead us to believe that this grace of the "baptism in the Holy Spirit" is meant for the whole church.

Baptism in the Holy Spirit is captive to no camp, whether liberal or conservative. Nor is it identified with any one movement, nor with one style of prayer, worship or community. On the contrary, we believe that this gift of the baptism in the Holy Spirit belongs to the Christian inheritance of all those sacramentally initiated into the church.[6]

This conclusion represents the majority opinion of Catholic theologians and biblical scholars associated with this Renewal: what charismatics today call "baptism in the Holy Spirit" is a believer's conscious awareness of the power and gifts of the Holy Spirit that come through baptism and confirmation, which was normal for those who received these sacraments as adults in the early Church.

---

6. McDonnell and Montague, *Fanning the Flame*, 9–10.

Baptism in the Spirit in Light of Classical Catholic Theology

Early in the Renewal, some theologians sought to understand baptism in the Holy Spirit in light of classical Catholic theology. In his 1974 book *Catholic Pentecostalism*, René Laurentin refers to a section of St. Thomas Aquinas' monumental *Summa Theologiae* in which St. Thomas explains the nature of the "invisible sending" or "mission" of the Holy Spirit:

> Such an invisible sending is especially to be seen in that kind of increase of grace whereby a person moves forward into some new act or some new state of grace: as, for example, when a person moves forward into the grace of working miracles, or of prophecy, or out of the burning love of God offers his life as a martyr, or renounces all his possessions, or undertakes some other such heroic act. (cf. *Summa* I, q. 43, a. 5, ad 2).[7]

Gregorian University's Fr. Francis A. Sullivan, in a 1982 book, concluded,

> It is quite in accord with traditional Catholic theology for baptized and confirmed Christians to ask the Lord to "baptize them in the Holy Spirit." What they are asking him for, in the language of St. Thomas, is a new "sending" of the Holy Spirit, which would begin a decisively new work of grace

---

7. René Laurentin, *Catholic Pentecostalism*, trans. Matthew J. O'Connell (New York: Doubleday, 1977), 44–45.

in their lives. As we have seen from the examples which St. Thomas gives, he would obviously not be surprised if such a new work of grace involved a charismatic gift.[8]

However, is the situation of most baptized Catholics today that of people already living a Christian life in the power of the Holy Spirit but ready to move into a "new state of grace" that would open them to working miracles, prophesying, renouncing all their possessions, and even being martyred out of love of God? Or is the actual situation that most Catholics *don't* really understand or experience a transformed life resulting from a personal relationship with Jesus and daily responsiveness to the Holy Spirit as the normal "fruit" of the sacraments of baptism and confirmation?

Dr. Ralph Martin poses this question, and he thinks that the latter is normally true. Contemporary baptism in the Spirit, he says, might correspond to what St. Thomas Aquinas describes in the *Summa Theologiae* (III, qq. 66–71): even when the sacraments are validly conferred, there may be many obstacles to the fruit of these sacraments coming forth in a person's life. Lack of faith, lack of understanding or desire to live a new life in Christ,

8. Sullivan, *Charisms and Charismatic Renewal*, 72. As Dr. Ralph Martin has observed, "Another strong proponent of the approach taken by Sullivan is Fr. Norbert Baumert, SJ, who has published books and articles supporting this viewpoint and was a main advisor to the German bishops' statement on the Charismatic Renewal. Norbert Baumert, "'Charism' and 'Spirit-Baptism': Presentation of an Analysis," *Journal of Pentecostal Theology*, Vol. 12, No. 2 (April 2004): 147–79. Ralph Martin, "A New Pentecost? Catholic Theology and 'Baptism in the Spirit,'" *Logos* Vol. 14, No. 3 (Summer 2011): 40.

lack of repentance, and even demonic influences may block the fruitfulness of the sacrament. The problem is not in the sacrament (which always confers grace *ex opere operato*), but in the lack of full consent, understanding, or openness in those who receive the sacraments (*opus operantis*). Aquinas acknowledges that the fruitfulness of these sacraments may vary considerably because of this. But Aquinas also teaches that those who desire more of the Lord can and will receive more of him, as Jesus taught: "Ask, and it will be given you; seek, and you will find" (Luke 11:9).[9]

St. Hilary of Poitiers, a doctor of the Church, wrote in his *Treatise on the Blessed Trinity,*

> We receive the Spirit of truth so we can know the things of God. . . . This unique gift which is in Christ is offered in its fullness to everyone. It is everywhere available, but it is given to each man in proportion to his readiness to receive it. Its presence is the fuller, the greater a man's desire to be worthy of it.[10]

This *foundational* movement of God's grace, Martin posits, is what happens most often today when one is baptized in the Holy Spirit:

> What most validly initiated Christians experience in this renewed actualization of baptism and confirmation is something they have never experienced before and simply "brings

9. See Martin, "A New Pentecost?", 29–34.

10. Lib. 2, 1, 33. 35: PL 10, 50–51. 73–75.

them up to code," as it were, with the beginnings of the Christian life as depicted in the New Testament. For most people baptism in the Spirit does not normally launch them from a base of fervent Christian life to a new and higher state or ministry or special calling; it is the activation of at least some of the basic fruits that the New Testament attributes to Christian initiation.[11]

An Eschatological View of Baptism in the Spirit

Another perspective is offered by Catholic theologian Msgr. Peter Hocken, who proposes that John the Baptist's statements about Jesus baptizing with the Holy Spirit and fire have an eschatological context; that is, Jesus' coming with the Holy Spirit and fire refers to the breaking in of God's kingdom in the final age of the world, and this great worldwide outpouring of the Holy Spirit today may be an "anointing" for the final proclamation of the gospel to the nations (see Matthew 24:14) preparing for the Second Coming of Christ. Although we do not know the "day or that hour" of Christ's coming (Mark 13:32), as the Catholic Church has always taught, it cannot be denied or dismissed lightly that in the past century, millions of people have come to believe in Jesus in a full and intimate way through the grace of the baptism in the Holy Spirit. This is certainly a sign that we are living in a time of mercy and grace that is preparing people's hearts to receive

---

11. Martin, "A New Pentecost?", 30.

the gospel through faith, which will help ready the world for the Lord's return, whenever that might be.[12]

Baptism in the Spirit as Revelation

Baptism in the Spirit may also be understood as a type of revelation—not the "public revelation" of Sacred Scripture and Sacred Tradition, nor the "private revelation" of an apparition, but a "personal revelation" of what it means that "Jesus is Lord." St. Paul taught that "no one can say [and by this he implies "know"] 'Jesus is Lord' except by the Holy Spirit" (1 Corinthians 12:3).

Catholic Scripture scholar Fr. Francis Martin defines baptism in the Holy Spirit as "a revelation made by the Holy Spirit to the Spirit of the believer that Jesus Christ is Lord." He continues,

> Many mature, well-balanced Christians can attest that their Christian life began seriously at the moment in which they were baptized in the Spirit. . . .
>
> Such people can also testify that this grace has grown in such a way that they now have faith conviction and assurance concerning the true identity of Jesus Christ. . . . The grace of Baptism in the Holy Spirit is thus understood to be knowledge

12. See Peter Hocken, "Baptized in the Spirit: An Eschatological Concept," *Journal of Pentecostal Theology* 13, no. 2 (2005): 257–268. Cited by Ralph Martin in "A New Pentecost?", 26, 41.

of Jesus Christ, power for overcoming sin, and conscious use
of the spiritual gifts in order to build the Body.[13]

Some people attest that their experience of baptism of the
Holy Spirit was not a "revelation" of Jesus, but something else,
such as a sense of peace or joy. Fr. Martin notes that, even in
those situations, if

> one perseveres in fidelity to this grace, one is unfailingly
> brought to a living awareness of the source of this grace,
> namely, our Lord Jesus Christ. That is, though our imme-
> diate perception might not lead us to assert "that the Lord
> has shown himself to me," upon reflection, we can see that,
> no matter what the original experience might have been, this
> was indeed the case.[14]

How does this happen, that an initial experience of peace,
joy, freedom, or a new spiritual gift invariably leads one closer
to God in Jesus Christ? In my experience, most of those who
receive this grace of baptism in the Spirit have a greater desire
to draw closer to God through prayer, reading Sacred Scripture, going to Mass and receiving Holy Communion (if they
are Catholic), and seeking the support and fellowship of those
who have had a similar experience. In all this, they find or are
confirmed in their belief that the source of their "new life" is

13. Francis Martin, *Baptism in the Holy Spirit: A Scriptural Foundation*
(Steubenville, OH: Franciscan University Press, 1986), 49–50.

14. Ibid., 21.

indeed the Lord Jesus Christ. Those who are baptized in the Holy Spirit through the prayers of other Christians have been told that Jesus is the one who "baptizes with the Holy Spirit" (cf. Matthew 3:11; Mark 1:8; Luke 3:16). So when something good happens as a result of the prayer "Jesus, pour out your Holy Spirit upon me," they believe that Jesus has answered their prayer. And if Jesus has the power to change their lives in that way, he has a rightful claim to be the Lord of their lives. It is as simple as that.

However, being baptized in the Spirit—a personal experience of the love and power of God—does not automatically make a person a better Catholic or a better Christian. That requires a decision and an ongoing yielding to God's grace. God's ultimate desire is our sanctification (cf. 1 Thessalonians 4:3). Francis Martin points out that there are three aspects of the grace of the baptism in the Holy Spirit: "deepened conscious awareness of the reality and presence of Jesus" (the "revelation" aspect); "an exercise of the gifts" of the Spirit; and sanctification. "The conscious presence of the Holy Spirit within the life of the believer is the foundation for cooperation with the Holy Spirit's action eliminating sin and bringing a person's life in order."[15] The ultimate test of the benefit of baptism in the Spirit is the fruit that it bears in a person's life and the life of the Church. As Jesus taught, "You will know them by their fruits" (Matthew 7:20).

---

15. Ibid., 48–49.

the WORD among us®

The Spirit of Catholic Living

This book was published by The Word Among Us. Since 1981, The Word Among Us has been answering the call of the Second Vatican Council to help Catholic laypeople encounter Christ in the Scriptures.

The name of our company comes from the prologue to the Gospel of John and reflects the vision and purpose of all of our publications: to be an instrument of the Spirit, whose desire is to manifest Jesus' presence in and to the children of God. In this way, we hope to contribute to the Church's ongoing mission of proclaiming the gospel to the world so that all people would know the love and mercy of our Lord and grow more deeply in their faith as missionary disciples.

Our monthly devotional magazine, *The Word Among Us*, features meditations on the daily and Sunday Mass readings, and currently reaches more than one million Catholics in North America and another half million Catholics in one hundred countries around the world. Our book division, The Word Among Us Press, publishes numerous books, Bible studies, and pamphlets that help Catholics grow in their faith.

To learn more about who we are and what we publish, log on to our website at www.wau.org. There you will find a variety of Catholic resources that will help you grow in your faith.

Embrace His Word, Listen to God . . .